Structuralism and Educa

Studies in Teaching and Learning
General Editor
Denis Lawton, B.A., Ph.D.
Professor of Education and Director
University of London Institute of Education

In the series:

Denis Lawton *An Introduction to Teaching and Learning*
John Robertson *Effective Classroom Control*
Maurice Holt *Evaluating the Evaluators*
Richard Aldrich *An Introduction to the History of Education*
Denis Lawton *Curriculum Studies and Educational Planning*
Edwin Cox *Problems and Possibilities for Religious Education*
Rex Gibson *Structuralism and Education*
Richard Pring *Personal and Social Development*
Patrick D. Walsh *Values in Teaching and Learning*
Maggie Ing *Psychology, Teaching and Learning*

Structuralism and Education

Rex Gibson

HODDER AND STOUGHTON
LONDON SYDNEY AUCKLAND TORONTO

British Library Cataloguing in Publication Data

Gibson, Rex
    Structuralism and education.—(Studies in teaching
    and learning)
    1. Structuralism
    I. Title   II. Series
    149'.96   B841.4

ISBN 0 340 33975 6

First published 1984

Photoset by Rowland Phototypesetting Ltd,
Bury St Edmunds, Suffolk
Printed and bound in Great Britain for
Hodder and Stoughton Educational,
a division of Hodder and Stoughton Ltd,
Mill Road, Dunton Green, Sevenoaks, Kent,
by Biddles Ltd, Guildford, Surrey

Contents

Studies in Teaching and Learning		vi
Preface		vii
Acknowledgments		viii
1	What is Structuralism?	1
	Notes	12
2	The Origins of Structuralism	14
	Notes	29
3	Structures of Thought	30
	Notes	44
4	Structures of Society	47
	Notes	59
5	Structures of Feeling	61
	Notes	86
6	Structuralism and Literature	88
	Notes	103
7	Structuralism and Education	105
	Notes	134
8	Structural Analysis	136
	Notes	153
Bibliography		155
Index		163

Studies in Teaching and Learning

The purpose of this series of short books on education is to make available readable, up-to-date views on educational issues and controversies. Its aim will be to provide teachers and students (and perhaps parents and governors) with a series of books which will introduce those educational topics which any intelligent and professional educationist ought to be familiar with. One of the criticisms levelled against 'teacher-education' is that there is so little agreement about what ground should be covered in courses at various levels; one assumption behind this series of texts is that there is a common core of knowledge and skills that all teachers need to be aware of, and the series is designed to map out this territory.

Although the major intention of the series is to provide general coverage, each volume will consist of more than a review of the relevant literature; the individual authors will be encouraged to give their own personal interpretation of the field and the way it is developing.

Preface

This book emerged out of a more wide-ranging project on social understanding with which I have been engaged over the past eight years. In that project I have explored some of the complex relationships between schooling, literature and society. What quickly became evident to me was that structuralism afforded valuable fresh perspectives in the study of education. My intention in this book is to show something of the nature of the structuralist enterprise and to indicate ways in which its contribution can fruitfully enlarge and advance educational studies.

Structuralism possesses much relevance for teachers as mention of some major writers who have employed its concepts shows: Jean Piaget, Basil Bernstein, Raymond Williams. These, and other less familiar scholars (for example, Ferdinand de Saussure, Claude Levi-Strauss), afford to teachers further opportunities to understand more clearly the social, intellectual and ideological contexts of schools and classrooms. As such, structuralism has important contributions to make to the reconceptualisation of the study and practice of education.

As the following chapters show, I am not uncritical of structuralism and its practitioners. It is a difficult and demanding mode of thought which uncomfortably challenges certain common-sense assumptions of teachers who have grown up in the British (rather than European) tradition. For example, in its preference for structures, its apparent devaluation of the individual is particularly uncongenial. I have therefore, in the method of *structural analysis* I develop in this book, attempted to remedy what I see as structuralism's major defects. Particularly I am concerned to restore human capability and knowledgeability to the centre of any analysis of schools and classrooms, and so, through this notion of human competence, help reduce the theory-practice gap. Structural analysis' four-fold structures of *competence, thought, feeling* and *social organisation* thus offer to teachers a method of using structuralist concepts in order to deepen their understanding of practice and hence improve it.

Cambridge, 1983   Rex Gibson

Acknowledgments

I am grateful to Miss Joyce Skinner, CBE, formerly Director of Cambridge Institute of Education, and the Governors of the Institute for affording me the opportunity of the study leave from which this book arose. I am also indebted to the present Director, Mr Howard Bradley, and the Secretary of the Institute, Mr John Child, for their active support during the writing of this book. I owe a particular debt to Professor Denis Lawton, Director of the University of London Institute of Education, for his interest, encouragement and advice; without his help the book would never have seen the light of day. I owe thanks also to my colleagues and students at Cambridge Institute (particularly Mrs Wendy Clarke now of Kingsleigh First School, Bournemouth) who have borne so tolerantly with my structuralist preoccupations over the past few years and who have made constructive criticisms of my use and interpretations of the method. My particular gratitude is due to the Library staff of the Institute, especially Mrs Lynne Taylor, who have performed minor miracles in obtaining promptly every one of my many library requests, and to Mrs Ivy Sheldon whose genuine interest in the project sustained me as she typed and retyped successive drafts with unfailing cheerfulness and efficiency.

1 What is Structuralism?

Introduction

In the spring of 1981 the University of Cambridge washed some of
its dirty linen in public. What quickly became known as 'the
McCabe Affair' variously intrigued, delighted, appalled, per-
plexed or amazed members of the University and outside obser-
vers alike. An Assistant Lecturer in the Faculty of English, Dr
Colin McCabe, was not upgraded to the post of University Lecturer, and the consequence of that decision by the Appointments
Committee sparked off what can only be described as an acrimo-
nious row. One of the many elements in the controversy was
structuralism, which McCabe was held to practise and teach.
Inside and outside the University privately and in public, com-
mentators on the McCabe Affair showed the depth of feeling that
mention of structuralism arouses. Students' 'minds were being
poisoned'; 'degeneration [was seen] happening week by week';
'their fiercely elitist intellectual movement is . . . a philosophy of
human poverty'; 'impenetrably obscure', 'congeries of nonsense',
'a passing folly', 'this bogey-man', 'odious and invalid' were some
of the terms used. More subtly, and in a style that has all the
hallmarks of 'Cambridge Wit', one critic remarked:

> I can, for example, say quite grammatically, and, what matters more,
> truthfully, that not all members of the Faculty of English are brushed
> with the same tar. If you see one or other of them smeared with a gooey
> black substance, you should not assume that he has rubbed against
> some structure or structuralist. He may be a perfectly honest man.[1]

What is structuralism? What is it that arouses such intense
feelings and conflicting assessments? Every writer who has
attempted to define it agrees, initially, on one thing: the extreme
difficulty of definition because of its many different forms. For

example, Jonathan Culler, a leading literary structuralist, remarks:

> One cannot define structuralism by examining how the word has been
> used; that would lead only to despair.[2]

And Edmund Leach, at once a critic and practitioner of structuralism in social anthropology, asserts that:

> Structuralism is a current intellectual fashion and the word itself has
> come to mean different things to different people.[3]

But for all its difficulty it is possible in this first chapter to gain an initial insight into structuralism in three ways: by citing actual examples of structuralist practice; by noting the range of application of the structuralist enterprise; and by setting out its distinguishing characteristics.

Some Examples of Structuralist Practice

1   First, from an essay on the face of Greta Garbo by Roland
     Barthes, a prominent French structuralist critic of the
     1960–70s.

> Garbo still belongs to that moment in cinema when capturing
> the human face still plunged audiences into the deepest ecstasy
> . . . Garbo offered to one's gaze a sort of platonic Idea of the
> human creature, which explains why her face is almost sexually
> undefined . . . many actresses have consented to let the crowd
> see the ominous maturing of their beauty. Not she, however;
> the essence has not to be degraded, her face was not to have any
> reality except that of its perfection, which was intellectual even
> more than formal. The Essence became gradually obscured;
> progressively veiled with dark glasses, broad hats and exiles:
> but it never deteriorated . . . Garbo's face represents this fragile
> moment when the cinema is about to draw an existential from an
> essential beauty . . . when the clarity of the flesh as essence
> yields its place to a lyricism of Woman. Viewed as a transition
> the face of Garbo reconciles two iconographic ages, it assures
> the passage from awe to charm. [In contrast] the face of Audrey
> Hepburn, for instance, is individualised, not only because of its
> peculiar thematics (woman as child, woman as kitten) but also
> because of her person, of an almost unique specification of the
> face, which has nothing of the essence left in it . . . As a

language, Garbo's singularity was of the order of the concept, that of Audrey Hepburn is of the order of the substance. The face of Garbo is an Idea, that of Hepburn, an Event.[4]

2 Next, from Claude Levi-Strauss, the leading proponent of structuralism in social anthropology. In his huge, four-volume study of myth we read:

> [Consider] the analogy between this natural product (honey) and menstrual blood. Both are elaborated (transformed) substances which result from a kind of infra-cooking, vegetable in one instance . . . and animal in the other. Furthermore, honey can be healthy or poisonous, just as a woman is a 'honey' when she is in her normal state, but secretes a poison when she is menstruating. Finally, we have seen that, in native thought, the search for honey represents a kind of return to nature, imbued with an erotic appeal transposed from the sexual to the gustatory register, and which would sap the very foundations of culture if it lasted too long. Similarly, the custom of the honeymoon would be a threat to public order if husband and wife were allowed to enjoy each other indefinitely, and to neglect their duties towards society.[5]

3 If these first two examples seem puzzling and unfamiliar, consider next a structuralist statement known to everyone:

$$2 + 3 = 5$$

4 Next, from the late Jean Piaget, who for all teachers is the best-known, most respected and most influential psychologist (and an out-and-out structuralist), two short extracts: the first concrete and clear, the second abstract and difficult, but both, essentially structuralist:

> (a) If a child is shown a piece of string bent at a right angle and one 'leg' A is progressively shortened, the child understands perfectly well that the other, B, thereby gradually becomes lengthened; only, for him this does not mean that the piece of string as a whole, A plus B, remains constant in size, because he estimates lengths ordinally, in terms of terminal points; for him 'longer' is the same as 'farther away', he does not count unit intervals. And though this piece of string does not, for him, have a constant length, it is nevertheless the 'same' piece of string throughout.

(b)   [In the growth of intelligence] we find the same functional
factors and structural elements. The functional factors are
assimilation, the process whereby an action is actively
reproduced and comes to incorporate new objects into
itself . . . and *accommodation*, the process whereby the
schemes of assimilation themselves become modified in
being applied to a diversity of objects. The structural
elements are, essentially, certain *order* relations . . . subordination schemes . . . and *correspondences* . . . As the
primary assimilation schemes become mutually coordin-
ated ('reciprocally assimilated') certain equilibriated
structures, those that make for a modicum of 'reversibility' become established.[6]

5   Structuralism and linguistics are deeply interconnected,
possibly because structuralism had its origins in linguistic
study (as we shall see in Chapter 2). Rather than choosing an
example from Chomsky or Jakobson, my extract comes
from John Lyons' discussion of a structuralist conception of
vocabulary:

Consider how we might translate into French . . . The cat sat on
the mat . . . How do we translate *the cat*? As *le chat*, knowing
that the animal being referred to was a male or being ignorant of
or unconcerned with its sex? Or as *la chatte* knowing that it was
female? The fact that French will use *chatte* in reference to a
female cat, known to be female, whereas English will not
necessarily use a phrase like *tabby cat* in the same circumstances
means that the distinction between *cat, tom cat*, and *tabby cat* in
English does not match the distinction drawn between *chat* and
chatte in French at any point . . . Consider, now, the translation
of *mat*. Is it a door-mat we are referring to (*paillason*), or a
bedside mat (*descente de lit*), or a small rug (*tapis*) . . . there is a
set of words in English, *mat, rug, carpet*, etc., and a set of words
in French, *tapis, paillason, carpette*, etc.; and none of the French
words has the same meaning as any one of the English words.
Each set of words divides a certain part of the universe of
domestic furnishings, as it were, in a different way; the two
systems of categorisation are incommensurate . . . what we do
when we translate is to determine, as best we can, how the
objects, events, and processes being referred to would be
categorized in terms of a more or less similar, but frequently
incongruent, system of distinctions and equivalences.[7]

6   Next an example of structuralism in science:

> One of the things I learnt when I was an aircraft engineer during
> the war was that if a control system has a time delay in the
> feedback loop – that is, if some time elapses between a control
> action and its effects on the object to be controlled – then the
> system is likely to oscillate. Consequently, whenever I come
> across a system which is oscillating, whether it be the menstrual
> cycle or the number of hares and lynxes in Canada, I look for
> delayed feedback. In doing so, I am assuming that structure
> determines behaviour. That is, if the components of a system
> are related to one another in particular ways, then the system
> will behave accordingly. The behaviour is determined by the
> structure, and not by whether the components are electrical
> circuits, hormones or animals.[8]

7   Finally, but by no means exhaustively, an example of
structuralist practice in education. Basil Bernstein is best
known for his work on language. Even in his earliest
writings on elaborated and restricted code, structuralist
influences can be clearly seen at work. In the 1980s he has
fully adopted structuralist methods. Whether conducting
an abstract discussion or applying his concepts to schooling,
his writing is (more obviously than any of the examples
given above) utterly (and often defeatingly) structuralist.

> . . . the unit for the analysis of codes is not an abstracted
> utterance nor a single context but relationships *between* con-
> texts. Code is a regulator of the relationships *between* contexts
> and, through that relationship, a regulator of the relationships
> *within* contexts . . . a code must generate principles for *disting-
> uishing* between contexts and principles for the *creation and
> production* of the specialised relationships within a context.
>   We can regard the social division of labour of a school to be
> composed of categories of agents (transmitters and acquirers)
> and categories of discourses ('voices'). If the coding principle is
> one of strong classification, then there is strong insulation
> between educational discourse ('voice') and non-educational
> discourse ('voices'). Discourses are strongly insulated from
> each other, each with their own specialised 'voices' so that
> transmitters and acquirers become *specialised categories* with
> *specialised* 'voices'.[9]

These seven examples of structuralist practice may seem an
unlikely and bewildering collection. What have they in common?

What is it that connects their heterogeneity? Before attempting to answer these questions I must briefly draw attention to the *range* of the structuralist enterprise and to a major reason for its neglect and undervaluation in England and other English-speaking countries.

The Range of Structuralism

The examples above show that structuralism encompasses a vast range of human experience. Little falls outside its orbit as it addresses itself to linguistics, anthropology, literature and literary criticism and the rest of the expressive arts, psychiatry, psychology, architecture, the physical and natural sciences, social science, mathematics, Marxism, philosophy, and certainly education. To claim that all such endeavours fall within the compass of structuralism is to make a very grand claim indeed, for it appears to elevate structuralism into a super-theory or super-method which holds the key to the explanation of all human conduct. But to recognise its far-ranging claims and applications is at once to alert us to its similarities with other all-inclusive theories (notably Freudianism or Marxism). Like these, structuralism comes in a very large number of versions, each with its own proponents claiming the superior truth and power of their own particular brand. Again, like Freudianism and Marxism, it is an explanatory *system*, made up of very abstract and elastic ideas, for which scientific precision is often claimed. In its confidence and all-embracingness it appears to answer a fundamental human need for order and coherence. The system that is structuralism comprises a variety of theories and methods which, by argument, assertion and evidence, advance claims to universal truth. But, once more like Freudianism and Marxism, the truths asserted are fiercely contested by schismatics and nonbelievers. What is clear however is that it cannot be ignored by teachers or by any other educated person. The seriousness of its challenge, the intellectual calibre of the contributions of its leading figures, make it a necessary topic for study. In this book I shall show something of its possibilities and limitations in a number of areas, and, particularly, how it offers fresh insights into educational theory and practice. Used selectively, its methods and concepts can aid evaluation and lead to improvement in schooling.

If structuralism *is* so important, why is it not a part of the furniture of most English minds? One major source of resistance and antagonism towards structuralism can be identified in its geographical origins and practice: it is European, or, more specifically, French. To say this is not to be xenophobic, it is to draw attention to the very different intellectual climates that characterise England (and much of the English-speaking world) and western Europe. The English cast of thought is pragmatic, empirical, commonsensical, suspicious of 'theory', very distrustful indeed of theory for the sake of theory. (Most teachers will recognise themselves in such a description.) That preference for practicality has deep and varied roots – for example, where the seminal philosophical contributions of Hume and Locke interconnect with the success of science in the practical achievements of nineteenth century industrial England. In contrast, 'theory' enjoys far greater prestige on the near-Continent. To become an 'intellectual' in France is to achieve at once a recognised and honoured status. In England no scholar or teacher could describe himself or herself as an intellectual without an acute sense of embarrassment. (If an Englishman was so insensitive as, without embarrassment, to so describe himself, the embarrassment (and amusement) among his hearers would be greatly heightened.) In brief, 'ideas' enjoy greater prestige abroad than they do among the English, who tend to root them in practice ('doing' is preferable to thinking). Structuralism is thus frequently uncongenial to the English mind, for it places a premium on ideas; it is often uncomfortably or unfamiliarly related to practice, to concrete instances and to empirical demonstration; and it employs and generates new concepts, new words. It is not surprising therefore that – Piaget apart – structuralism is little known and suspiciously regarded. It is against this background that the neglect of structuralism in courses for teachers has to be understood. My strong conviction is that teachers need to acquaint themselves with cultures other than their own, or those of education and schooling. There is an urgent need to tap alternative currents of thought and feeling, to range outside the customary preoccupations of student teachers or teachers themselves. To do so offers fresh insights and different perspectives on everyday practice. The challenge of multiculturalism is all too slowly being taken up, but at least it is now acknowledged. Structuralism as a method has not yet entered the consciousness of most teachers. Yet the variety of thought and practice that is structuralism affords intellectual refreshment and potentialities for changed, enriched practice. It may look strange, it may at first be intellectually uncongenial, but it can provide genuinely revealing linkages with what is already known and felt. It throws fresh light on familiar practices, and, in its creation of

altered perspectives, can enable the transformation of those practices.

What is Structuralism?

In spite of its sheer variety it is possible to identify the key ideas
shared by all types of structuralism. Most fundamentally, its
central notion is that certain basic structures (or systems or
symmetries) govern and explain any object of study. The object of
study may be the human body, the human mind, society itself,
language or literature, mathematics, mythology, the natural
world, or indeed, any phenomenon. Underpinning this central
conception are six related ideas, all of which can be detected in
some form in the seven examples of structuralist practice given
above.

First, the notion of *wholeness*: the assumption that the whole is
greater than the sum of the parts. Thus, for example, in human
biology, heart, lungs, liver, brain, and so on, do not simply *add up*
to the human body; rather, the body is a functioning whole to
which all these elements contribute. They work and are to be
understood with reference to the body, something that is not an
aggregate but a whole. The elements are subordinated to laws and,
as Piaget puts it, 'it is in terms of these laws that the structure, *qua*
whole or system is defined'. Such laws are not reducible to the
relations of the elements but to their relations with the whole.
Society, then, is more than the individuals who comprise it;
language more than the words contained in a dictionary;
mathematics more than its numbers. In '2 + 3 = 5' the integers do
not exist in isolation, but are understood by their structural
properties, by their relationships to the system that is number. In
example 6 above, the overriding importance of *wholes* is made
utterly explicit: the scientist assumes 'that structure determines
behaviour,' *not* the components of a system or structure.

Directly following from the notion of wholeness is the second
characteristic of structuralism. Reality lies not in things (i.e. units,
components, elements or parts) but in the *relationships* between
them. Again, to take a physical example, the liver is known by its
relationship with other organs and the body as a whole. Only in
these relationships can the liver be understood; as a 'part' its
significance and meaning lie in its relationships to things outside
itself. Or, to take a language example, a word is known only
through other words, by its setting in language. We understand

the meaning of a word, say the structuralists, by reference not to *itself* but to the totality that is language. In the same way that the number 2 is to be understood by its relations in a system, so too structuralism shifts attention in social matters from individual to society: the individual is a 'part', society a 'whole'. The individual is to be understood, and gains his meaning and significance from, the web of social relationships in which he exists. Alone, isolated, a 'part', whether organ, word or individual, has no significance or meaning, for significance and meaning can only arise from the context in which that part is embedded: body, language and society respectively. When Bernstein, in example 7 above, states that 'the unit for the analysis of codes is not an abstracted utterance nor a single context but relationships *between* contexts' he makes evident this structuralist assumption: *relationships*, not *things* are the proper focus of structuralist attention.

The third characteristic at once becomes clear. It is less an idea or concept of structuralism than a consequence of the two elements just described. In the technical language of structuralism it is expressed as 'decentring the subject'. Put more simply, this means that man (or woman) loses his (her) place at the centre of things; from 'man the measure of all things' he becomes an element in a system, where elements have less significance than the totality. No longer is *man* the proper study of mankind, but the *whole* that is mankind itself. The individual is to be explained by reference to that whole, and thus becomes subsidiary to the whole. This 'decentring the subject' can be seen as a characteristic development of the modern world: part of that long process which includes Copernican astronomy, Darwinian biology, the physical sciences, Comtian sociology, late Marxism, Freudian psychology. However unlike structuralism they may be, all are evidence of such 'decentring', for each pushes man away from centre stage, explaining him within a larger, universal system. The focus of attention shifts to that system which gives meaning and existence to its elements. This uncongenial, controversial (and, for many, unacceptable) feature of structuralism demands that just as the word must give way to language, so man must give way to society. Often it is this apparent rejection of the human individual that so provokes antagonism to structuralism. In the 'human' examples given above we can see Garbo and Hepburn yielding to essence and existentialism; Levi-Strauss' men and women and Piaget's child in thrall to necessary, unrelenting structures of mind; Lyons' translator struggling within given, incongruent, language systems; and, for Basil Bernstein, the human subject – pupil, teacher, boy, girl – is at the mercy of that supremely structuralist concept: 'code'. In similar fashion the scientist is not interested in the individual lynx or hare, but in the system which contains them.

Self-regulation is structuralism's fourth characteristic. The whole, the system, is held to maintain itself, to make for closure, to govern its elements such that they change, if required to do so, to ensure the preservation of the totality. There is what could be called a homeostatic feel about this characteristic which asserts that through the application of rules or transformation laws or functions, the system's survival is ensured. Examples include the rhythmical mechanisms of the body (eating, sleeping, and so on), a language's incorporation of new words or change of use of old ones, and such social practices as the incest taboo or *rites de passage*. In each case the system (body, language, society) uses its elements to maintain itself. Thus the system manages its own changes, its own transformations, but always according to its own laws. This self-maintenance and closure is most clearly seen in '$2 + 3 = 5$' where the addition of two numbers yields a third which satisfies the laws which generate it. Neither the closure nor the self-maintenance which are the characteristics of self-regulation are to be thought of as restricting or impoverishing but as enriching.[10] In example 4 above, the Piagetian functions of accommodation and assimilation are the self-regulating mechanisms for intellectual growth (see Chapter 3 for an explanation of these concepts). In the Garbo example, essential beauty yields to existential beauty in the cinema's treatment of the female face.

Fifth, structuralists prefer the *snapshot* method. To use their own technical language, they assert the primacy of *synchronic* analysis over *diachronic* analysis. All such technical terms mean is that study of a language, or a society, or the human mind, is best conducted by examining the relationship of parts *at a particular moment*, rather than studying its development over time. Thus, the preferred method is that of a snapshot, rather than a moving film; history is of little importance, what matters are the relationships *now*. The origin of this preference is in the work on language of Ferdinand de Saussure (discussed in the next chapter). Although the preference may seem an unusual one, it is in fact a familiar practice in many areas of schooling. Mathematics is undertaken essentially synchronically ($2 + 3 = 5$), so too is much science. And in English studies, anyone who has engaged in the practical criticism of a poem has undertaken synchronic analysis: an examination of how the parts relate to each other, how meaning and significance reside in the text itself. I. A. Richards in his seminal book *Practical Criticism*[11] reports how he presented poems devoid of all context to undergraduates for analysis. As such it can be seen as an exemplar of synchronic analysis (although Richards cannot be labelled a structuralist). This apparent devaluation of history is another crucial source of antagonism towards structuralism (particularly by Marxists). In each example above, the preference for explanation by way of a snapshot of the system is evident.

Finally, a key idea of structuralism is *transformation*. Such an idea appears to contrast strangely with preceding characteristics which suggest that structuralism is essentially static in its preference for synchronic analysis and self-regulation. But these do not necessarily conflict with the notion of transformation, for the latter draws attention to those laws of wholes that themselves constitute the origin and direct the flow of change. Such laws are both structured and structuring: that is, they allow a dynamic between part and part, part and whole. In that dynamic, change is a necessary consequence. As Piaget puts it: 'all known structures . . . are, without exception, systems of transformation'. Structures then, are subject to change, but according to the laws of system. The notion of transformation is clearly seen in structuralist approaches to language. It is the assumption that directs the search for the deep structures of language, and is particularly evident in Chomsky's notion of transformational grammar.[12] Structural linguists, whilst remarking that languages are almost infinitely varied and undergo change over time, posit the existence of universal rules or laws governing those differences and changes. Similarly, sociologists and anthropologists seek the structural rules or principles which underly the widely different manifestations of the social practice they study. Societies change, but their transformations are to be explained by appeal to structural laws (for example of kinship or relations of production). Similarly, mathematics or biology can be seen most fundamentally as systems of laws of transformation. In $2 + 3 = 5$ the transformational nature of mathematics is self-evident. In each of the other examples given the notion of transformation is equally central (e.g. in Barthes' 'the cinema is about to draw . . .'; in Levi-Strauss' 'transformed substances'; in Piaget's 'assimilation' and 'accommodation'; in Lyons' 'translate'; in science's 'determined'; in Bernstein's 'generate' and 'creation and production').

These then are the general characteristics of structuralism. It can be seen that utterly central is the notion of *wholeness* or *totality*, with its attendant assumptions that meaning inheres in rela-

tionships not things, and that laws of self-regulation and transformation are characteristics of structures. Structuralism then is
both a theory (or rather, theories) and a method.

At this stage it would be a valuable exercise for the reader to
check his/her grasp of structuralism by considering each example
given above and trying to detect in each the characteristics I have
set out in this chapter. An appropriate summary is provided by
Robert Scholes:

> At the heart of the idea of structuralism is the idea of system: a
> complete, self-regulating entity that adapts to new conditions by
> transforming its features whilst retaining its systematic structure.[13]

In this chapter I have shown something of the nature and
practice of structuralism and illustrated the objections it arouses. I
have identified some of the reasons why it is found so uncongenial
by many orthodox scholars, and will raise further criticisms as the
focus is sharpened in subsequent chapters which will examine its
origins in the writings of Saussure and its subsequent development. We will then be in a position to see how it can contribute
powerfully to the study and practice of education.

NOTES

1   A full account of the two-day discussion of the Senate of the
    University of Cambridge can be read in the *Cambridge University
    Reporter*, 5108, CXI, 18, 18 February 1981. Other analyses of, or
    comments on the affair, particularly with reference to structural-
    ism, appear in *The Times Literary Supplement*, 6 February 1981
    ('Modern Literary Theory'); *The Guardian*, 14 February 1981 ('The
    Oxbridge Malaise'); *The Observer*, 1 February 1981 ('Structuralism
    and Dry Rot'). All quotations are taken from one or other of these
    sources. The Cambridge affair however was merely a sharp, local
    manifestation of a continuing highly acrimonious disagreement. In
    1983 the tone of the argument remains bitter and shrill: 'grievance
    and paranoia', 'establishment conspiracy', 'the book is no good',
    'absurd', 'a peculiarly masculine species of pornography': see Tom
    Paulin (1983) *London Review of Books*, 5, 2, p. 5.
2   Culler (1975). Jonathan Culler's book is seminal in British literary
    structuralism.
3   Leach (1973). Sir Edmund Leach, former Provost of King's Col-
    lege, Cambridge, is an anthropologist who has played an important
    role in structuralist analyses of other cultures.

4 Barthes (1972a, pp. 56–7).
5 Levi-Strauss (1978, pp. 412–13). Claude Levi-Strauss is the fore-
   most structural anthropologist. His work is examined in Chapter 3.
6 Piaget (1971, pp. 63–5). As we shall see in Chapter 3 this book is
   important for all teachers wishing to grasp the nature of the
   structuralist endeavour. It should be treated with some caution as it
   is very uncritical of structuralism.
7 Lyons (1973, pp. 5–19).
8 Smith (1982, p. 12).
9 Bernstein (1982, p. 304).
10 See Piaget (1971, p. 14).
11 Richards (1929). More than half a century later Richards' book still
   merits the closest attention of *all* teachers – not only teachers of
   English.
12 Chomsky (1965). Noam Chomsky's contribution to structural linguistics is examined in Chapter 3.
13 Scholes (1974, p. 10). Scholes' book is an easy introduction to
   structuralism in literature although it has been largely superseded
   by Culler's (1975) more demanding text.

2 The Origins of Structuralism

The origins of structuralism lie in linguistics: in the work of Ferdinand de Saussure (1857–1913). He must be acknowledged as structuralism's founding father albeit in a rather curious fashion. He himself 'wrote nothing of general significance',[1] not even the book for which he is known (and from which structuralism springs). The *Course in General Linguistics* was published after his death from notes taken by students who attended his lectures at the University of Geneva between 1907–11.[2] There is an appealing irony in the fact that it was only through the commitment and energy of his students that this modest, even obscure, professor has become entitled to take an equal place beside his exact contemporaries, Freud and Durkheim, in effecting a revolution in twentieth century thought. It seems likely that Saussure knew little or nothing of the work of Freud or Durkheim, but, like them, his stress on unconscious phenomena and on structural explanation has transformed how we view psychic processes (Freud), society (Durkheim) and language (Saussure).

Saussure's work represented a reaction to nineteenth-century linguistics that had stressed the historical study of language: the search for its roots and a patient tracing of the development and changes in meaning of words. For such history he was to substitute the snapshot (synchronic) method, a concern to study the whole of language at one particular moment in time. Further, he was to turn away from a commonsense theory of meaning (where the meaning of a word is referred to a particular object) to emphasising the relationships between words in the totality that is language. His work, though essentially concerned with language, has major implications for the study of all aspects of human behaviour, not least, as I shall show, education and schooling. In this chapter we will examine his key ideas: ideas which have informed the development of structuralism in its many forms. I shall discuss them under five headings: *langue and parole*; signifier–signified; the arbitrary character of the sign; difference; synchronic versus diachronic analysis. Although for many readers these may be new terms and hence all too easily dismissed as jargon, it is vitally necessary to grasp the meanings and significance these technical impressions imply. I can readily understand (and indeed share) readers' suspicion of neologisms, but the *ideas* of Saussure are of fundamental importance. The terms serve initially as convenient shorthand.

Saussure's Key Ideas

(a)   *Langue* and *Parole* (language and speech)

Saussure's primary concept is his emphasis on the difference between *langue* and *parole* (language and speech).[3] He asserted the supremacy of the totality, *langue*, over *parole*, pointing out that all speech derives from language and is given meaning by it. Language is not simply the total of words that exist, such as might be found in a dictionary; rather, it is a system, a whole, a body of rules, independent of any speaker, historically given, upon which speakers are forced to draw. It is a system of relationships between elements, and any element (a word, an utterance, *parole*) is defined by its position in language as a whole. *Langue*, then, a system of rules, makes *parole* possible: I can speak (or write, or interpret what I read or hear) only because of my grasp of *langue*. And that knowledge, as we shall see, is mainly subconscious.

Speech or *parole* exists in the here and now, and is experienced in linear form, as one word follows another. It is an *event*, made concrete in time and space. Language (*langue*) has no such linear form, is never visible. It is an abstract whole, comprised of relationships, and constituting certain stored cognitive capacities. It is the corpus of knowledge upon which each speaker draws to produce the unique statements that are *parole*. *Langue* is system; *parole* is any realization (or expression) of that system. For Saussure, the linguist's primary task was to study language as a whole, to map its rules and relationships, to discover its nature and form. In his emphasis on language as a whole can be seen a very different approach from that of Wittgenstein and Searle, whose focus of study is the speech act itself. *Langue* for Saussure is primary, *parole* secondary.

If all this sounds rather abstract, a non-linguistic analogy may help. When you watch a football or cricket match, what you see most vividly, concretely, is the equivalent of *parole*: Kevin Keegan scores a goal, Ian Botham hits a six. These events are immediately present before your eyes, they are familiar, immediately understandable (as well as being intensely exciting). But what enables you to understand what you see – and, indeed, what directs or explains Keegan's or Botham's actions – are the non-visible, abstract, rules of the game: that 'whole' which is football or cricket itself. Here is a social equivalent of *langue*. Keegan and Botham, both supremely gifted individuals, work within a system, a structure; in their every action they draw on that structure, express it, realise it. They act (scoring goals or runs) and comprehend what they are doing, in the context of a structure which existed before they were born and will exist long after they have stopped playing: the rules of the game. This is not to say those rules are fixed for all time; of course they change, and some of the transformations are due to the actions of uniquely gifted individuals. But the structures that are football or cricket enclose, contain, motivate and explain the actions of these unique individuals. Botham hitting a six is an *event*, we experience it within a structure. And when I write these sentences and you, the reader, read them, these are events, *parole*; but I write them and you read them through the structure that is *langue* (a structure of which we both have a very firm understanding, and yet, paradoxically of which we could give only the sketchiest, faltering account). We know far more than we can say.

What is quite clear is that Saussure's *langue–parole* distinction is the counterpart of the *whole-part* relationship noted in Chapter 1 as the primary characteristic of structuralism. But it is important to emphasise that there is a crucial difference from, say, the organ-body relationship of biological structures. In biology, both whole and part appear to be present for our examination, we can actually see both body and organ. In *langue–parole*, only *parole* is ever present, *langue* is always absent. A sentence or a word exemplifies language, witnesses its existence, but language itself can never be present, is never seen, can never be grasped as a whole. Dictionaries are not *langue*, but a form of *parole*, for language is the whole complex of relationships, never physically graspable in its totality. Indeed, to make this point is to show how misleading the biological organ-body analogy is, for the 'whole' in that case is not simply the physical body which we can see, but the (absent) relationships of organ-body which we cannot. And, in the same way, it would be a mistake to think that the rules of the game of football or cricket are simply those which we can hold in our hand as a published document.

The relationship then of *parole* to *langue* is one of *presence* to *absence*, a distinction which has been made much of by later structuralists. The existence of *langue* is implied in every speech or writing act, in presences, as the words are heard or seen; but it is understood in *absences*, through the rules of language which are never fully made manifest. In the twentieth century, linguists have accepted Saussure's challenge to identify and analyse these rules and relationships, but for all their efforts only a small fraction of Saussure's vision of *langue* has been charted.

The *langue–parole* distinction is a crucial one not simply for linguistics, but for understanding all social life. The football and cricket analogy above illustrates its importance. Contemporary sociologists increasingly emphasise how individuals draw upon a totality of social knowledge, which acts as a *resource* as well as a *restricter* for human action. Like language, this stock of social knowledge is held as a complex set of stored capacities, and are realised by, and instantiated in, every social action.[4] It is this totality, never clearly visible, that gives meaning to any particular action. The importance of the *langue–parole* analogy for schooling and education is evident. Any classroom event (John adding numbers; Mary pushing John; Mrs Jones the teacher speaking to Mary) has to be understood within a structure, or rather, as I shall later make clear, structures. John, Mary and the teacher are unique individuals, their personalities and actions are concretely, particularly, self-evidently their own, but the insight Saussure provides is that we must seek adequate explanations of their conduct – and possibilities for change – in those non-visible structures that comprise *langue* and its equivalents. Similarly, Saussure's concept of *langue–parole* relationships can provide fruitful insights into any discussion of curriculum, or school ethos, or evaluation, or other matters of relevance to education (see particularly Chapters 7 and 8).

Before moving on to other concepts, I must at once make two related fundamental criticisms of Saussure's *langue* and *parole*. First, what is all too obviously lacking here, as from structuralism itself, is the notion of the competent individual. The priority given to *langue* (structure) over *parole* (event) neglects the relationship of the two, for the connecting term that articulates *langue* with *parole*, structure with event, is the individual. This is evident not simply by thinking of Botham or Keegan, but by considering almost any human action. The very act of speaking is itself a demonstration of human competence: a grasp, albeit intuitive, unconscious, taken-for-granted, of the structure that is *langue*. Young children, as well as adults, seen in this way, provide dazzling displays of such competence. This leads to the second critical point: both *langue* and *parole*, like structure and event, should be seen to be *incursively related*. Thus, the totality gives meaning to the particular, but also the particular (*parole* or event) draws upon, revivifies, recreates and eventually transforms the hidden, absent, totality (structure, *langue*). When a pupil says 'The Normans conquered England in 1066' his apparently straightforward utterance is at once evidence of the complex structures of language, time (1066), place (England) and society (Normans), on which he draws, and of their revival and recreation through human agency. It is the necessity of grasping this essentially incursive relationship, this reciprocity of *langue* and *parole*, structure and event, general and particular, group and individual, that I am concerned to stress in this book. In my view, the priority structuralism gives to *langue* neglects this reciprocity.

(b)   Signifier–signified

Saussure's view of language was that it is a system of signs. This may seem banal, but it has been of vital importance to our understanding both of language and all social action. To say that language is a sign system is to assert that speech or writing are basically signs, that is, noises or marks on paper which express and convey meaning. Without meaning they are merely noise or marks, not language. As Jonathan Culler puts it, noises count as language only when they serve to express or communicate ideas; otherwise they are just noise. This draws attention to the fact that a sign system is a system of conventions and language a particular set of conventions about meaning. In this system Saussure distinguishes between the *signifier*, the sign itself (the word/letter/sound) which is the vehicle of meaning; and the *signified*, which is the idea or meaning conveyed.

Saussure's emphasis on the sign and on its component elements, signifier and signified, has resulted in a new discipline: *semiology*. It was Saussure's explicit wish to establish 'a science of signs', and for him semiology would be

a science which studies the life of signs in the heart of the life of society . . . (telling us) in what signs consist and what laws govern them.

Such a discipline would not be restricted to linguistics, but would study all forms of communication in society such as rites, forms of politeness, military signals. Although the development of semiology has taken writing and speech as the fundamental signifiers, it has been characterised by its concern to construe everything as sign systems (dress, actions, food, and so on), in short to construct a semiological study of culture. The extract in Chapter 1 by Roland Barthes on Garbo's face (pages 2-3) is an example of semiology.

Schooling is a potentially rich field for semiological study and its neglect is an interesting feature of educational studies. Not only does the study of signs have direct curriculum relevance for the study of films, television, advertising, but schools themselves abound in signs: conventions which convey meaning. School uniform, a pupil raising his hand, rewards and punishments are obvious examples; the timetable, the grouping of pupils, the subjects of the curriculum, the written information provided to parents, parents' evenings . . . indeed any school activity can be seen as a sign system and so available to semiological analysis. The *signifiers* are evident everywhere, the *signifieds* are necessary and complex items for investigation. When a first-year pupil in a comprehensive school is handed his timetable on his first day at his new school, the piece of paper he clutches in his hand is a signifier. He spends the rest of his school career making sense of that document; these 'signifieds', and those of his classmates, teachers, parents are the vital and legitimate objects for any research which is concerned to aid understanding and change of schooling.[5]

Structuralist use of signifier–signified runs counter to Anglo-Saxon common sense and is a frequent source of confusion and hostility. For it is important (and, for many, initially bewildering) to realise that Saussure uses the technical expressions, signifier and signified, in an attempt to break free of a common-sense theory of reference. That is, neither concept refers to 'the thing itself': *signifier* is the word or sound, *signified* the concept. His argument is that when you say 'dog' you do not refer to an actual object, a dog you can actually see: an object 'out there' in nature. His use of *signifier* is an attempt to show that meaning comes not from reference to an object but from the position of a word in relation to other words. Meaning, for Saussure, derives from the system of *langue*, from its formal relationships and rules, and not from its relationship to an outside, independent world. This is a very unfamiliar, uncongenial notion for many readers but the importance of the signifier–signified distinction becomes clearer in considering the next element in Saussure's theorising.

(c)   The arbitrary character of the sign

Most of us take for granted that when we say 'dog' we mean good old Rover, whom we can actually see before us. Not so for Saussure. His concern was to shift the reference of a word away from an object in the natural world to its meaning within the total communication system of language itself. Meaning, for him, arose not from objects, but from the relationships of signs. He insists therefore on the *arbitrary character of the sign*. This does not simply mean that there is no intrinsic relationship between a word and the object to which it refers but, in Saussure's terms, no intrinsic relationship between signifier and signified.

An everyday example demonstrated his claim: the word 'tree' has only an arbitrary relationship with the object itself, for it can be rendered as 'tree', 'arbre' or 'Baum' depending on which language is used. It could equally be called 'rudd' if all speakers in a community so agreed. Only convention links the word with the object; there is no logical, necessary connection. And only convention links signifier and signified, word and concept. For Saussure the relation is arbitrary or 'unmotivated'; the meaning of a word comes from its relationships with other words, from that complex sign system, itself an 'absence', the totality that is *langue*. The concept itself, all that comes into our mind as we hear or read the word 'tree', had, for Saussure, no independence, no separate existence. The concept, the thought (signified), like the word (signifier), is an element in a language system, and is given meaning by that system. Once again we see how structuralism's 'wholes' are dominant over elements.

In this insistence on the arbitrary character of the sign we see the revolutionary character of Saussure's scheme. He proposes a radical break in the relationship between language and the world, wishing to split off language from any external reference. The meanings that human beings seek are to be found, he insists, in the system of language itself and not in the external world, for any words which refer to that world have only an arbitrary connection with it.

The implications of this divorce of language and reality are profoundly disturbing for teachers for it seems to go against common-sense assumptions: is 'naughty' behaviour no more than that behaviour which (some) teachers have agreed to label as 'naughty'? Are 'standards' merely the arbitrary assertions of particular groups? Are 'special needs' merely social constructions of professionals (Tomlinson, 1981, 1982)? Is there no essential core of meaning in 'education' but only conventionally agreed elements? If Saussure's assertion of the arbitrary character of the sign appears dangerously relativistic we should recall Juliet's much earlier 'What's in a name? That which we call a rose/By any other name would smell as sweet', or Hamlet's comment on morality 'For there is nothing either good or bad but thinking makes it so.' But Shakespeare, unlike Saussure, was not concerned to sever language and reality. The latter's endeavour in, for example, 'the cat sat on the mat' is not just to show that 'the' and 'on' and 'sat' are to be understood by the system that is language, but so too, such seemingly objective, identifiable words as 'cat' and 'mat' are similarly grasped by reference to language, rather than to 'things' we can see.

Three uncomfortable consequences of Saussure's claim follow. First that no sign ('naughty', 'standards', 'pupil' and so on) carries meaning on its own: it has meaning and significance only as part of a system. Second, that systems or structures (e.g. schools, societies, languages) may be – to use a technical term – incommensurable: that is, they may not be 'translatable' (see example 5 in Chapter 1, page 4). Naughtiness for one group is simply not naughtiness for another; the standards of one group may be dis-valued by another.[6] Third, language is elevated into the supreme definer of reality; a view equally uncongenial to 'practical' Anglo-Saxons, to Marxists, and to any underdog. None of these three consequences can be dismissed simply by appeal to common sense. All three demand sustained examination by teachers and others. But here, to further grasp the notion of the arbitrary character of the sign, we must examine how, through the concept of 'difference', Saussure argues the relational nature of language.

(d)   Difference

Saussure's 'arbitrary character of the sign' and his notion of the totality of *langue*, arise from his insistence that

In language there are only differences *without positive terms*.

Using a distinction that would later become the pivot of Levi-Strauss' work, he argues that meaning arises out of *oppositions*, from differences in particular contexts. Thus, red is what is not yellow or green, it is defined by its relationships within the colour system, not by itself. Similarly, it is in the differences arising from the relational qualities of language, not in the isolated words themselves, that differentiations, categories, boundaries, give meaning:

> Signs define one another neutrally by means of their differences from one another . . . 'The' and 'this' are meaningful only in so far as they are implicitly distinct from 'a' and 'that'.

Here, once again, we see the structuralist insistence, noted in Chapter 1, on relationships rather than substance, concepts depend on other concepts, they are not free-standing, independent, autonomous, but are totally dependent on the system. In Saussure's memorable phrase, 'their most precise characteristic is that they are what the others are not'.

Using the example of the 8.25 Geneva–Paris express, Saussure argues that it is not the *content* (i.e. particular objects: the carriages and engine) that makes it the Geneva–Paris express. Rather it is its itinerary, structured as the timetable of places and times, that give it its identity and meaning and makes it different from all other trains. It is differentiated from other trains by its timetable and although it may leave late or early, have more or fewer carriages, it is always the 8.25 Geneva–Paris express. Its *form* not its content gives meaning, and that form is given by what it excludes, that is, by its place within a whole system.

This emphasis on meaning deriving from context, from differences, is somewhat similar to Wittgenstein's ideas on chess. In that game meaning is purely internal, embodied in its own rules, and rules and moves are understood as a system of relationships. Ability to play is defined as knowing what to do in a particular context. Thus, some totality or whole that is 'chess' governs each particular piece, move or sequence. The form rather than the content is dominant as the differences between the pieces constitute the game. A piece itself may be of any size or shape: but its identity inheres in its difference from other pieces within the 'whole' that is the rules of chess. As Jonathan Culler puts it 'identity is wholly a function of differences within a system'.

A simple language example illustrates Saussure's argument. The word 'pan' means very different things to a cook, a theatre critic, a goldminer, a Greek scholar, a camera man, a maker of sanitary ware. Standing alone it has no meaning, for its meaning derives from the context in which it is used and its differences from other words within that context. When Saussure argues that language has no positive terms, he is saying that it is constituted by internal oppositions, and that a concept or word is, paradoxically, what other concepts or words are not. This is not an easy idea to grasp or accept, but it identifies language as a series of internal relationships that allow speech to be generated. Every speaker knows these relationships (as their ability to speak testifies) as part and parcel of the tacit knowledge that enables everyday life to take place. Just what the relationships are is a deeply complex and hotly disputed affair.

If the notion of 'difference' is a challenging one in language, it becomes even more problematic and contested in social and personal matters. For it asserts that 'pupil' or any other role is to be understood not as commonly accepted: a social position, a 'thing', a role we can actually see an individual playing, but rather as a relationship, graspable (and playable) only by reference to other roles, its most essential feature being its difference from other elements in the structure of schooling. And questions of personal identity are raised in their sharpest form if the Saussurian argument prevails: are *you* most crucially, most significantly, 'what the others are not'? Emotionally, intellectually, culturally, we reject such a negative definition. Here we see decentring of subject at full stretch. If Saussure's structuralism is encouraging because it stresses interdependence, relationships, intelligibility (Piaget's 'affirmative ideal'), it is profoundly subversive to notions of individual identity or autonomy as conventionally understood. It is not simply the abstract nature of 'difference' which makes it uncongenial and distasteful to the English mind. But yet . . . What Saussure's concepts provide are tools for thorough exploration of the whole range of practical school experience.

(e)   Synchronic–diachronic analysis

We have met synchronic and diachronic perspectives in Chapter 1. Saussure's interest in them arose from his concern about how linguistic study should be done. Synchronic analysis, the method he favoured, is like a snapshot: taking language at a particular point in time and studying its relationships as a series of oppositions. It studies the structure of language at one moment in its history. Diachronic analysis concerns itself with how language changes; it is the study of language evolution over time. Synchrony and diachrony then are about method, and Saussure's endeavour was to reject the diachronic analysis favoured by nineteenth-century linguists.

Saussure's preference for synchronic analysis may seem strange, particularly so as he acknowledged how words change over time. For example: the word 'silly' has passed from 'blessed, pious', through 'innocent, helpless' to its present 'foolish, stupid'. However, the apparent paradox is easily explained. He wished to distinguish between the language *system* and linguistic *evolution*. It was because of his insistence on the arbitrary character of the sign, and because of his acknowledgment that words do change in meaning over time and between cultures, that he argued that there is no necessary core or essence in the sign *itself*. What the radical historicity of language actually demonstrates is the absence of any essential core of meaning. Once again, we see the structuralist emphasis on relations not things. A sign is simply relational, and the crucial relationships are the ones that obtain at a particular moment. It is just because signifiers and signified *do* change ('cattle' once meant *any* property), are arbitrary, that they require snapshot treatment, for the snapshot best shows the relevant relationships. Language, for Saussure, 'is a system of pure values (concepts) which are determined by nothing except the momentary arrangement of its terms'. History becomes irrelevant, and past meanings are no help in understanding present usage. Knowing the history of the words 'silly' or 'cattle' may be of some interest, but it is unnecessary to understanding the function and meaning of the words in modern English. Those functions and meanings are given by the current structures of language.

There is no space here to detail the subtleties of Saussure's arguments for synchronic analysis of language. The matter is still hotly debated by linguists. It is when we turn to the social applications of his principle that the preference for synchrony becomes even more disputable. To neglect history in the study of schooling seems shortsighted, even foolish. For Marxists, historical analysis is central and thus another element in their fierce rejection of structuralism. Yet many studies of classrooms, not structuralist, but in the ethnographic tradition, seem almost wilfully to take schooling out of history, to concentrate on the here and now interaction of individuals without taking account of the structural and historical pressures which shape present action.[7] Although Saussure's theories of language are particularly fruitful for social analysis, his synchronic preference seems very difficult to defend. The historical development of schooling, social class and politics is of crucial relevance to understanding present-day educational processes. My own view is that, to some extent, history may be 'read out of' a snapshot. Current classroom practices reveal, in part, some of their antecedents. The past is contained in the present. But direct appeal to history yields a fuller, less inferential, picture.

Saussure: Challenge and Criticism

Ferdinand de Saussure's thought, painstakingly reconstructed by his students, has had a profound influence on twentieth century intellectual life. In linguistics, anthropology, literature, sociology, psychology and many other fields, the radical challenge he posed to common-sense, taken-for-granted assumptions has resulted in exciting, controversial developments, often ill-received by prevailing orthodoxies. His difficult, subversive views have found both enthusiastic adherents and vehement opponents. His severance of language from external reference, his stress on the arbitrary relationship of signifier and signified, his non-historicity, and his insistence on relationships and differences, represent in effect the creation of meaning out of non-meaning. In arguing that individual terms mean nothing alone, but that they have meaning only within the totality, and in his concept of language as a system of signs, he is at once the founder of structuralism and semiology. What is particularly interesting is that his ideas, flowing from the *langue–parole* distinction, can be located in an intellectual movement (in its loosest sense) that includes very disparate thinkers and subjects: Wittgenstein's 'language games'; Gadamer's concept of 'tradition'; Kuhn's analysis of 'force' in Newtonian and Einsteinian physics; modern mathematics.[8] All these endeavour to show how the totality of associations explain individual parts, rather than vice-versa. They evidence the shift in emphasis from substance to relations. So too, as I shall show in Chapter 5, do those developments in literature and the arts we label 'modernist'. The paintings for which Picasso is best known, for example, or cubism, or the writings of James Joyce or Samuel Beckett, similarly celebrate form over substance, relationships over things.

We should note too how the 'decentring of the subject' found in such recent, and to most English teachers, unfamiliar writers such as Jacques Lacan, Louis Althusser, Jacques Derrida, or Roland Barthes is prefigured in Saussure's linguistics.[9]

That decentring has posed a major challenge to the few certainties left to man as religion has been progressively undermined as the sure basis of knowledge and practice. In our modern secular world those certainties were available largely through the philosophy of Descartes and the sure knowledge that science could provide. In both these worlds, philosophy and science, the human subject, the irreducible 'I', is firmly at the centre, guaranteeing certainty. The Cartesian certainty, *Cogito, ergo sum*, and empiricism, with its firm belief that knowledge is derivable from one's own senses, both rest on the assumption: what can be more sure than my knowledge of myself? And the very notion of individualism, at the heart of English bourgeois culture, enshrined the belief as common sense. Structuralism shakes this certainty as it 'deconstructs' 'I' as an element in a superior structure.

Saussure and the structuralism that followed him effected a Copernican revolution in human affairs. Just as Copernican astronomy pushed man's Earth from the centre of planetary activity, so too structuralism displaces subjectivity, man himself, to the edge of the social system. The human subject becomes the end result of the process, not its origin. The decentring of man was the consequence of Saussure's attention to the modes in which meaning is created in and through language. Structuralism was to emphasise and apply this principle to all human activity. Far from 'I' being personal and the most certain knowledge, structuralism asserts that 'I' only makes sense in relation to the totality of language and hence of society. All personal expressions, 'I', 'you', 'me', 'they', have sense only through our 'insertion into language'. So, for structuralists, 'I' is not an innocent term, but is a consequence of the totality of language and the social. Meaning resides not in the word or person, but in associations within the whole. When Levi-Strauss speaks of 'the insertion of the human being into a totality of linguistic signifiers' he is displacing 'I' as the fundamental term of what it is to be human, and calling rather for explanations in terms of signifying properties of language. Self can only be found within a totality, in relationships. There is no real, true self that transcends history, context. Proust's quest was a mistaken one, for there is no pristine self lying behind the social, waiting to be discovered. For teachers (to whom the notion of personal identity is central) such ideas present particularly acute and uncomfortable problems which must be faced and grappled with. We cannot afford to rely simply on the comfortable rhetoric of bourgeois individualism to secure our own and our pupils' uniqueness. Structuralism's theories and its investigations in other fields provide fruitful but neglected methods and findings to enable us to undertake in fresh if unfamiliar ways the study of how personal identity is formed in the interaction of structure and individual.

But Saussure's ambitious programme has serious defects as its major failure of realisation has demonstrated: the mapping of the relationships that constitute *langue* remains little more than a theoretical dream. Some of the reasons for this failure can be quickly identified. Most important is structuralism's apparent inability to grapple with the problem of relativity. The insistence on the arbitrary character of the sign deprives the theory of the possibility of reference. Put simply, if language is assumed to have nothing other than arbitrary links with an external world, it becomes impossible to speak of any truth outside the closed system that is language. In severing the link between language and the world, in insisting on the primacy of relations over substance, of form over content, the Achilles' heel of structuralist theories is immediately evident, for there is no means of adjudicating the truth of different descriptions, claims, assertions. All descriptions – and all moralities – become equally valid. Bad (or good) behaviour is no longer possible. Further, translation or interpretation of different cultures becomes wellnigh impossible, for the assumption of a closed system of language within each simply avoids such issues. There is, for example, a self-defeating feel about writing on education which assumes that middle-class teachers and working-class pupils inhabit quite different universes and are incapable of understanding each other. Without denying all the problems of different subcultures, or of multi-ethnic communities, the common, shared, experience and assumptions that schooling (and society) provides should not be overlooked.

A further problem to which I have already drawn attention is that Saussure's scheme disregards the existence of the competent language speaker. Saussure barely discusses what it is that connects *parole* to *langue*. This represents failure to see that the connection is human competence itself. By diminishing the individual to a mere part in a system ('decentring the subject') and by making that system the prime component in any explanatory scheme, structuralism effectively rules out human competence. It is curious that for all his stress on semiology, on man as meaning-endowing, always striving to make sense out of his surroundings, Saussure did not use this notion to link *langue* and *parole*. As Chomsky points out, language is more than a system of inter-related units: it is a system of rules, and such rules imply and demand competence of performance. He argues that there is no place in Saussure's scheme for 'rule-governed creativity' of the kind involved in the ordinary everyday use of language.

This failure to achieve an adequate dialectic between system and individual is one which I attempt to remedy by developing the method structural analysis in Chapter 8. All social life (and schooling is perhaps the most urgent and illuminating example) requires those who write about it to acknowledge human competence and in so doing to recentre the human subject and to reconceptualise his/her relationships with the structures in which he/she is embedded. Without the notion of pupils and teachers as competent, not only are descriptions and analyses of schooling seriously flawed, but possibilities for improvement of practice are radically reduced.

Criticism must also be made of the different criteria Saussure employed for separating *langue* from *parole* (essential from contingent; social from individual; psychological from material). Such fundamentally different methods of division have given rise to much controversy. And, as noted, Saussure's distinction between synchronic and diachronic and his preference for the former raise major problems both for language and social life. Synchrony (snapshot) depends on history, and constancy has sense only with reference to time. Saussure attempted to take language out of time, but such an attempt seems doomed to failure. The relationships observable between language elements at a particular moment have a past as well as a present, and that continuity must be taken into account in any satisfactory explanations of change. Such considerations have even more force when applied to social affairs.

Developments in linguistics since Saussure are not our concern, neither is the detail of the almost infinite variety of structuralist theories that have burgeoned from his seminal ideas. Rather, in order to show the relevance of structuralism to education, and to develop an approach which overcomes some of its difficulties, I shall examine, in the light of the characteristics identified in Chapters 1 and 2, the work of certain major thinkers who have employed or been influenced by structuralist methods and assumptions. The very organisation of the following chapters suggests the importance of structuralism for education, for their titles speak of the major concerns and activities of schooling: structures of mind, structures of social organisation, structures of feeling. After considering the particular instance of structuralism and literature (again, central to educational practice), I shall draw the themes together showing how my method of structural analysis can enliven and illuminate educational thought, and can offer to teachers not only fresh ways to understand and describe their practice, but also insights into ways in which those practices may be improved.

NOTES

1 Culler (1976, p. 9). Culler's book is an indispensable (if somewhat celebratory) introduction to Saussure.

2 de Saussure (1974).

3 The fact that the *Course in General Linguistics* was compiled from students' lecture notes, and not written by Saussure himself raises certain problems: e.g. Is it *sequenced* as Saussure would have preferred? Are certain topics (particularly *the arbitrary character of the sign*) given less attention than Saussure may have wished? Is the terminology of the editors sufficiently consistent? Jonathan Culler argues that Saussure's thought is best reconstructed by considering the *Course* in a different order from that published. My own preference is to begin, as does the *Course*, with a discussion of *langue* and *parole*. Readers should note that Culler would almost certainly disagree with me that *langue–parole* represents Saussure's primary concept – he argues for the primacy of the *arbitrary character of the sign*.

4 The work of Anthony Giddens (1976, 1977, 1979, 1981, 1982, 1983) is of particular importance. Although he is critical of Saussure's structuralism he acknowledges and utilises the power of its central ideas.

5 Mills (1978). This is an intensely enjoyable account of one ex-pupil's attempt to recall how he made sense of his school experience from the day he was handed his first-year timetable.

6 The 'untranslatability' of one culture into another has been a popular theme of recent sociology of education: pupils' perspectives and teachers' views of reality have been claimed to be not simply poles apart, but irreconcilable. See e.g. Willis (1977).

7 I am not thinking simply of the Open University text by Hammersley, M. and Woods, M. (eds) (1976). One of the weaknesses of the current 'teacher as researcher' movement is a neglect of the historical and structural setting of classrooms.

8 Gadamer (1975); Wittgenstein (1972); Kuhn (1962).

9 Barthes (1967); Lacan (1977); Derrida (1978); Althusser (1969). These writers have (or had) a profound influence on French intellectual life in the 1960s and 1970s but are little known in Britain. All four have been greatly influenced by structuralist ideas, but the work of each is very different in focus and character. A concise but somewhat curious examination of the links between these and other writers is in Kurzweil (1980).

3 Structures of Thought

Introduction

All teachers, because their task is to foster understanding, are centrally concerned with structures of thought. Most teachers are structuralists. The first assertion is unexceptional, the second surprising. In this chapter I shall examine the contribution structuralism has made to our knowledge of how we think: to structures of mind. This must involve consideration of the work of two leading structuralists who have devoted their lives to just that enterprise of mapping the structures of human thought: Claude Levi-Strauss and Jean Piaget. Mention of the latter name will alert the reader to the basis for my controversial assertion that most teachers are structuralists. Piaget has had an incalculable influence on nearly all teachers over the past fifty years. To the extent that they have absorbed his theories they are structuralists.[1]

If structuralism indeed 'seeks to discover principles of thought formation that are valid for all human minds' (as Piaget puts it) and stresses the primacy of these intellectual structures over social practices, then its roots stretch much farther back than Saussure. Plato, Kant and Hegel in their different explorations of cognitive structures, and in their preference for idealism (the predominance of the mental over the material) display structuralist characteristics. More recently, so too does *Gestalt* psychology. *Gestalt*, a German word for pattern or configuration or structured whole which is different from its elements, has come to characterise a school of psychology dating from the early years of this century whose leading figures were Kurt Koffka, Wolfgang Köhler and Max Wertheimer.[2] Although mainly experimental psychologists they applied their key concept (that elements are subsidiary to wholes and determined by them) to the arts, science and philosophy. For *Gestalt* theorists the human brain strives to organise perceptions and sensations into wholes: we hear music as a melody, not as individual notes; we seek 'good' form in what we see (simple, regular, symmetrical, closely packed and so on). Piaget has criticised *Gestalt*ists for their narrow definition of intelligent behaviour and for underplaying the activity by which humans construct structures, but their unmistakable structuralist emphasis comes through in the remark of Köhler who, significantly, trained as a physicist, and took his notion of 'field' (an organised whole) from that discipline:

> The very physiological process of our brains must be . . . in Maxwell's, in Planck's and in my *own* sense, structured, functional wholes.

Noam Chomsky's theory of deep structures of language can also be seen as an attempt to plot the structures of the human mind. His claim is that all human languages, although their 'surface structures' are different (for example, English and Chinese), must have a basic structure in common (deep structure) which corresponds to what might be called genetic programming. Starting from the astonishing fact that no one actually teaches a child language, but that young children learn it nonetheless, Chomsky argues that we must have a biological endowment which – in interaction with the environment – determines our mental and linguistic growth. The importance of this claim cannot be overstressed for, like Kant, he is asserting that anything that does not 'fit' this given structure of mind (i.e. anything that cannot be 'caught in its net') is both unintelligible and unexpressible: we can neither see, understand, nor say it, if it does not match our pre-ordained structures. In a striking analogy, Chomsky likens the development of language to the physical growth of arms and legs, or the advent of puberty:

> Language seems to me to grow in the mind, rather in the way familiar physical systems of the body grow . . . it's not inappropriate to regard the mind as a system of mental organs – the language faculty being one – each of which has a structure determined by our biological endowment.[3]

This model of the mind, genetically determined, might seem narrowing and constraining, but Chomsky is at pains to stress the richness of the biological endowment. Just as the mechanisms of generative grammar enable us to make infinite use of finite means, so too he argues that our genetic programme is so abundantly fertile that it enables us to think and act creatively, even freely.[4] The research inspired by Chomsky into the deep structures of language have so far yielded little conclusive evidence of their existence, but Chomsky's basic idea and the positive, humanistic, quality of his conception of the structuralist enterprise have both appeal and conviction.

Nonetheless it must be pointed out that Chomsky's structuralism has fierce critics who would certainly not agree with my favourable assessment in the preceding sentence. Ernest Gellner in one of his many criticisms of the structuralist endeavour singles out and condemns Chomsky's work because it disenchants and diminishes human power and capacity. He sees Chomskian structures as 'sinister' in their 'indifference' to human beings:

> Any explanation of human conduct or competence in terms of a genuine structure is morally offensive – for a genuine structure is impersonal, it is an 'it', not an 'I'.[5]

Brief mention must be made at this point of the work of the philosopher of education, Paul Hirst. Certainly not a structuralist, nonetheless his enterprise of sketching and detailing the structure of knowledge can be seen as a major contribution to our understanding of the structure of the mind. His basic conception of 'forms of knowledge' has strong affinities with both Kant and Chomsky; and, for teachers, has direct value and application to curriculum planning. Hirst claims that we interpret, make sense of our experience of the world, in certain ways. When he claims that these ways, 'forms of knowledge', are logically distinct, he is asserting that they correspond to the structure of our minds, the mesh or net of our thought. Thus, we can do no other than classify and understand our being in the world through our pre-given networks of concepts and truth tests which define the distinct forms. What are these forms of knowledge? Hirst identifies seven: the physical sciences, mathematics and formal logic, the human sciences and history, moral understanding, religion, aesthetics, philosophy. If Hirst's theory has validity its educational consequences have vital importance, for the teacher's task derives from this structure: to deepen pupils' understanding of each form and to grasp their differences.[6] What is certain is that all teachers of pupils of all ages must address themselves to the question of how children and adults think about the world, for these structures of thought and practical issues of curriculum construction and teaching method are indissolubly connected.

But it is the work of two self-acknowledged structuralists that must now be examined: Jean Piaget and Claude Levi-Strauss. These two are giant but contrasting figures of structuralist thought. Both are centrally concerned with structures of thought, but they differ in method, reputation and acceptance. Piaget's work is painstaking, empirical, prestigious, widely replicated; Levi-Strauss' is imaginative, speculative, controversial. Piaget has had a massive impact on primary teachers' practice for almost half a century; Levi-Strauss is virtually unknown to teachers.

Jean Piaget (1896–1980)

Piaget's interests embrace psychology, philosophy, linguistics and mathematics. He had set out, in an *oeuvre* encompassing sixty years, over forty books and countless articles, a comprehensive and detailed account of the nature and development of intellectual growth. In his best known (and most accessible) book on structuralism he examines the nature of mathematical, logical, physical, biological, psychological, and linguistic structures, together with structuralism in social science.[7]

Declaring himself a structuralist, Piaget sees rich possibilities in the method, viewing it as a positive affirmative ideal – the intrinsic intelligibility of structures – an intelligibility held in common by all structures, whatever their particular application. In this Piagetian view of structuralism we sense a reaction to the fragmentation of knowledge in the modern world and a concern for a coherent system that will at once unite and make sense of our diverse, often bewildering, experience. Piaget is the most forceful advocate of structuralism's orderly, affirmatory power. In language which expresses that affirmation of intelligibility he shows how it seeks coherence in the face of reductionism and fragmentation:

> For the mathematicians, structuralism is opposed to compartmentalisation, which it counteracts by recovering unity through isomorphisms. For . . . linguists structuralism is a departure from the diachronic study of isolated linguistic phenomena . . . and a turn to the investigation of synchronously functioning unified language systems. In psychology structuralism has long combatted the atomistic tendency to reduce wholes to their prior elements.[8]

Note Piaget's contrasts here: 'unity', 'unified' are preferred to 'compartmentalisation', 'isolation', 'atomistic'. In his own work on intellectual growth in children, Piaget displays all those features of structuralism noted in Chapter 1, but it is clear that, in his stress on the child as the active agent of his own growth, he does much to inject a theory of human competence that is so noticeably absent elsewhere. For Piaget, children 'construct' their structures of mind. But even here, that human activity is subject to controlling laws:

> Observation and experiment show as clearly as can be that logical structures are constructed, and that it takes a good dozen years before they are fully elaborated; further, that this construction is governed by special laws.[9]

There is, however, always a dialectic between individual and structure; intelligence develops through interiorized action as the child engages with his world. Piaget's emphasis on *construction* (which finds correspondences with Romantic theories of child development)[10] ensures that his work has become the scholarly lynchpin and justification of the progressive tradition of education. Always Piaget stresses the transformatory aspect of structure. He discovers a dynamic in the development of human intellect that ensures a *flow*, as the laws of composition of structured wholes guarantee both stability and change, emergence and transformation. Speaking of the period seven to ten years he writes:

> We are here in the presence of, and can even follow step by step, an activity of construction that yields genuine structures, structures which are already 'logical' and which are nonetheless 'new' when compared with those that preceded: the transformations definitive of the new structures grow out of the formative transformations, from which they differ only in equilibration.[11]

Piaget's model of mind then is a system of self-regulating, transformatory structures which develop through the activity of the child. There are excellent accounts given elsewhere of the details of his structuralist account of intellectual development in which all children pass through a sequence of stages that is held to be universal and invariant.[12] Only a very brief account of these stages and certain other major concepts is necessary here, together with an indication of some of the criticisms of his work.

Piaget's stages of intellectual development

> During any given stage many superficially different patterns of behaviour can of course be seen to occur. Underlying them, however, there is held to be some common structure which explains them and gives the stage its unity.[13]

1 *Sensori-motor Stage* (birth to eighteen months/two years approximately)

The infant constructs a notion of a stable world in which objects have a stable identity and existence in space and time independent of himself and his actions.

2 *Concrete Operational Stage* (eighteen months/two years to eleven years) with two sub-periods

(a) Pre-operational stage (eighteen months/two years to seven years) The young child develops the capacity to symbolise: to represent things to himself. Thought and language greatly extend his grasp of the world, but he is still closely tied to immediate physical objects concretely experienced.

(b) Concrete operations (seven to eleven years) Classificatory principles of number, type, time and quantity are greatly extended as are the concepts of reversibility and conservation. Although concrete experience is still central, symbolic action (language and thought) massively expand the child's ability to understand and explain the world.

3 *Formal Operational Stage* (twelve onwards)

No longer tied to immediate, concrete experience, the adolescent can reason logically, hypothesise, deduce consequences. Abstract thought enables the thinker at this stage systematically to coordinate his own classificatory principles. This stage, like all others, involves the child in the active reconstruction of his achievements at previous levels.

Underlying these stages of development are certain functional and structural factors. The functional factors are *assimilation* (where through the reproduction of an action, new objects are incorporated into existing structures), and *accommodation* (where schemes of assimilation are themselves modified to fit new situations). These two processes are complementary and inseparable and are observable at all stages of intellectual development ensuring both continuity and change. The structural elements are *order relations* (the order of movements in a reflex act, in an habitual scheme, in the suiting of means to ends), *subordination schemes* (the subordination of more simple schema to more complex ones), and *correspondences* (matching recognitions of many types).[14] Piaget throughout uses the notions of *groups* and *equilibrium* as structuralist concepts which (in a complex manner that can only be hinted at here) at once guarantee stability *and* transformations, continuity *and* variability, self-regulation *and* modification.

Piaget's structuralist account of the growth of intelligence is both monumental and infinitely subtle. Any brief account of it, as above, is little more than a caricature. But in recent years it has been subject to growing criticism. Its stages are often interpreted as being too clear-cut; it is frequently misunderstood by teachers to the detriment of pupils (see e.g. the telling criticism by Denis Lawton (1981) of 'readiness');[15] there is underplaying of the importance of social, emotional and motivational factors in his developmental scheme;[16] language, too, is curiously neglected, its influence on thought largely unexamined (even when Piaget did pay close attention to language, in his study of egocentric speech, his work is now generally seen to be largely mistaken). Further, recent research has shown young children to be more advanced in their thinking than the Piagetian scheme implies; and adolescents and adults certainly do not correspond exactly to the model of formal operations he proposes[18] – illogicality is common. Then, too, Piaget has been criticised for the conduct of his experiments, the nature of his evidence and his failure to consider alternative theoretical explanations. There are few explicit criticisms of his structuralism, but in the particular criticisms of, for example, his notion of *equilibrium* as a too all-encompassing and vague notion, can be detected an attack on the stress of wholeness and unity on which structuralism is based.

In spite of these criticisms Piaget exemplifies a variety of structuralism which has gained wide-spread acceptance and has had tremendous influence on the practice of education. In embracing his theories (however uncritically or inappropriately) almost all teachers in Britain and the USA who have trained within the past two or three decades are structuralists. His writings stand as a towering monument of structuralist achievement and, refreshingly, a structuralism that has been interpreted as stressing human, individual action.

Claude Levi-Strauss (1908–   )

Piaget's prestige sharply contrasts with the disputes that attend the structuralist theories of his contemporary, Claude Levi-Strauss. Piaget says of Levi-Strauss:

> Structuralism's most distinguished representative is the very incarnation of the structuralist faith in the permanence of human nature and the unity of reason.

Going further, he sees an intimate connection between his own theory of cognitive structure and Levi-Strauss' doctrine of the primacy of structure in social life, however different their methods of deriving such theories.

Like Piaget, Levi-Strauss has published extensively and his thinking is complex and difficult to grasp. Nonetheless, it is possible to specify precisely his main endeavour: the unconscious properties of mind that underlie the production of human cultural objects: 'the unconscious nature of collective phenomena'. His search is for structures of mind, for the universal structural characteristics of human thought; structures which are opaque or unknown to man himself. Thus the fundamental principle of Levi-Strauss's structuralism is that,

> all social life, however elementary, presupposes an intellectual activity in man of which the formal properties cannot, accordingly, be a reflection of the concrete organisation of society.[19]

Such stress on the priority of ideas over material relationships ('concrete organisation') is a dramatic reversal of Marx, and a return to the idealism of Hegel. It is therefore all the more surprising that Levi-Strauss acknowledges an intellectual debt to Marx, for much of his work is antithetical to Marxist versions of history and structure.

Levi-Strauss acknowledges certain other major figures whose thought has influenced his own. From Durkheim (particularly his *Elementary Forms of Religious Life*, and (with Mauss) *Primitive Classification*) comes the preoccupation with categories of thought and the search for how different cultures code the natural world. From Roman Jakobson the linguist comes the central concept in Levi-Strauss's structuralism: the stress on *binary oppositions*. Saussure is acknowledged for his emphasis on whole over part, structure over individual event, relationships over objects, and for semiology, the science of the signs. There is also a debt to Freud with his emphasis on the unconscious in culture and the search for universally valid principles of thought formation. And Rousseau's stress on language as marking man off from Nature is seen by Levi-Strauss as seminal in his own search for human universals and in his stress on the value of non-modern, non-Western cultures. Rousseau's influence can be seen as a critique of Western hegemony which, asserts Levi-Strauss, should be seen for what it is: domination that does not permit the possibility and authenticity of alternative 'primitive' styles of thought. Although Levi-

Strauss' work is unfamiliar to teachers, there is no doubt that his self-set task (to map the structures of mind), his mentors and his methods make him necessary reading for the fresh perspectives on education and schooling that his work can provide.

Given his abiding concern with the structures of human thought, Levi-Strauss' work falls into three stages. First is his preoccupation with the traditional anthropological problem of kinship. His work here is very controversial as he seeks, in a novel manner, the structures of kinship. Second is his concern to provide a theory of classification through a study of totemism. Here his problem is, how do primitive societies classify their world? From such classifications, he argues, can be derived universal structures of mind. Third is his abiding concern, the structure of myth.[20] The study of myth is particularly appropriate to his main endeavour for, like music, he believes it to express a *langue*, suppressing time, capable of an infinity of performances, and thus expressing universal qualities of mind.

Myth represents a good example of Levi-Strauss' structuralist method in its attempt to uncover the universal but unconscious properties of mind by which people in all cultures produce meaning. His claim is that there are a series of basic categories of mind which can be decoded through the examination of culture – in this case, myth. To avoid the problem of the relation of myth with history (a problem always present in the myths of Western society), he studies the myths of 'societies with no histories' – for example, tribal Brazilians and Australian aborigines. Such people live in what he calls 'cold' cultures (opposed to Western 'hot' cultures), where time is cyclical, not linear, and where writing is unknown. When myths from such cultures are analysed, behind the narration can be seen certain structures which serve as a code revealing the structures of the mind. Such structures arise out of *binary oppositions*, for Levi-Strauss argues that the basis of all differences are binary.

Leaving aside all the formidable problems that arise from the fact that these myths as we in the West come to know them are probably very different from, and certainly divorced from, the context of their original telling, Levi-Strauss asserts that the myths contain, under their surface content or meaning, a deeper meaning: a message expressed in code. His purpose is to decode that message. In passing we should note how similar this is to Freud's interpretation of dreams (with its attendant problem: how can it be proved to be true or false?). Leach describes his method as 'verbal juggling with a generalised formula . . . (leading) into a world where all things are possible and nothing sure' and he wonders whether it might not simply be 'clever talk'. In spite of such difficulties it is possible to give an outline of what Levi-Strauss is attempting. Taking a corpus of myths together, he argues that the various recurring themes (incest, patricide, matricide, cannibalism . . .) are coded messages resembling an orchestral score.[21] The message being passed is contained in this 'score', rather than in any particular myth, and the message invariably concerns itself with a binary opposition and an attempt to resolve the contradiction revealed. The function of myth is then seen to be to reveal and overcome such contradictions as life/death, this world/other world, man/gods, incest/exogamy, sexual intercourse/virgin birth. In each case the contradiction is founded on the dominant binary opposition of nature/culture.

A particular example illustrates his method. Discussing Greek myth, Levi-Strauss maintains that one contradiction needing resolution was their religious belief that man first grew from the earth (autochthonous) as against their knowledge that man was born of the union of man and woman. He uses the Oedipus myth as a logical tool to relate the original problem (born from one or born from two) to its derivative (born from different or born from the same).

> By a correlation of this type, 'the overrating of blood relations' (i.e. *incest*) is to 'the underrating of blood relations' (i.e. *fraticide, patricide*) as 'the attempt to escape autochthony' (i.e. earth-born) is to 'the impossibility to succeed in it' (i.e. born of *man–woman union*). Although experience contradicts theory, social life validates cosmology by its similarity of structure. Hence, cosmology is true.[22]

Such intellectual legerdemain, such sweeping generalisations, such imaginative *chutzpah* reminds us, as Leach remarks, of Alice *Through the Looking Glass*. But it clearly reveals the mathematical form of this reasoning in its use of binary oppositions (with incest/patricide generalised as 'overrating of blood relations'/ 'underrating of blood relations'). The thrust towards abstract, universal forms is clear. But the method lends itself to caricature, for when Leach examines a number of Greek myths he identifies 'the irresolvable unwelcome contradiction' that 'if Society is to go on, daughters must be disloyal to their parents and sons must destroy (replace) their fathers.'[23]

Such criticism has never worried Levi-Strauss who uses the method of binary oppositions to examine a vast range of cultural activities: cooking, making fire, diet, sexual practices. In all these he argues that form matters more than content, that the binary oppositions universally found create cultural meaning and significance. Such binary oppositions arise he claims because the human brain is structured into certain ordering mechanisms. These universal structures organise how man sees and apprehends the world, and they are evidenced in all cultural practices and artefacts: rituals, myths, objects. Because cultures are constructed by human minds, they reflect those minds. Even if cultural practices differ, as they do, common *structures* can be perceived which maintain the thesis of universal psychological structures.

These ordering mechanisms or structures of mind make us see the world as a series of differences, or, for Levi-Strauss, oppositions. Black is the opposite of white, man of woman, culture of nature and so on. This notion of binary opposition owes much to Levi-Strauss' fascination with the language of computers and to his association with Roman Jakobson whose linguistic analyses take a rigid binary form. Meaning derives not from the thing, the content, the singular feature (black, man, culture) but from its *relationship*, its opposition to something else. To take an example, consider the opposition of red and green. They are opposite in our perception of the colour spectrum, and are opposite in our signalling system (traffic lights: red-stop, green-go). In nature and in culture, therefore, the same *structure* is found: but the human mind goes further, for it seeks a mediating term to resolve the oppositions. In the colour spectrum we perceive yellow lying halfway between red and green; in traffic lights the sequence is red, yellow, green (stop, caution, go). Thus the human brain seeks binary oppositions in nature, but, dissatisfied with the resulting discontinuity or paradox, further seeks a mediating term to resolve or link those oppositions.

The identification of oppositions and mediating or transforming terms are presented in structuralist analyses as triangles; Levi-Strauss' culinary triangle is typical. In all cultures food is eaten either raw or transformed in some way (cooked or naturally rotted). The binary oppositions are thus culture/nature and normal/transformed.

Levi-Strauss has put a great deal of work into his culinary triangle, but the Anglo-Saxon mind finds it very difficult to take seriously the discussion of roasting, boiling, smoking and the mediating processes of air, water and receptacles. But, as Leach observes, 'behind the nonsense there is a sense', for anthropology reveals that very different cultures sort out their foodstuffs and apply status distinctions to it (roast beef is 'superior' to boiled

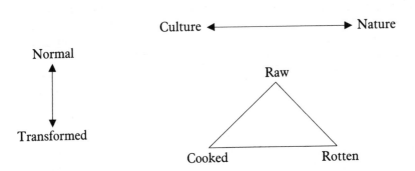

Figure 1   The culinary triangle of Levi-Strauss *Source:* Leach (1970, p. 30)

fowl) in remarkably similar ways. Levi-Strauss shows a singular capacity to identify binary oppositions: exchange/no exchange, receivers/givers, symmetry/asymmetry, alternation/repetition. Always he asserts that they arise from the nature of the human mind, and that the most powerful myths represent an unconscious attempt to overcome their contradictions. The Christian myth of the Virgin Birth is thus concerned with the oppositions sexual/ asexual, dirty/clean, sinful/sinless, wife/mother. All must be re-solved, and virgin birth is the prime mediating term to resolve such contradictions.

What is to be made of Levi-Strauss' structuralist claims that the mind is structured to decipher codes, that those codes are in the form of binary oppositions and that transformations are effected to resolve those oppositions? Although his theorising attracts great interest and among certain theorists enjoys much prestige as a fundamental contribution to our understanding of individual-society relationships, it is open to many criticisms.[24]

Much criticism concerns itself with the adequacy of the empir-ical foundation of Levi-Strauss' theories. By the standards of the Anglo-Saxon tradition of anthropology, the duration and nature of his fieldwork is extremely limited and sketchy. Further, his frequent citing of examples of cultural practices divorced and altered from their original context and form is regarded as a highly dubious practice. British anthropologists in particular see in his work the same undisciplined eclecticism that they note in Frazer's *The Golden Bough*. His theories are often regarded as being little more than imaginative speculations and interpretations, with examples chosen selectively to fit. Neither falsification nor proof seem appropriate in discussion of validity.

Levi-Strauss' notion of categories based on binary oppositions is particularly suspect, for such a fundamental reduction seems very unlikely to match the complexity of the human mind. Jakobson's original thesis has been virtually discredited, and a computer-type model of the human brain is almost certainly misconceived and outdated. It receives little support from Piaget's work which reveals the great complexity of children's thought structures. Rather than meaning arising from binary oppositions a theory that stresses *networks of contrasts* would more appropriately match the nature of human understanding.

Epistemological difficulties arise from the charge that Levi-Strauss has no mode of discriminating knowledge from ideology, for the contrasts invoked between Western and tribal societies' thought create a very specific problem of cultural mediation. Thus his claim to detect structural oppositions in myths is vitiated by the charge that such oppositions may simply be a consequence of *his* (Western) mind. He may be imposing modern, scientific structures of thought on primitive minds in which such structures are simply not present. This is not mediation, but cultural imperialism, and suggests that Levi-Strauss does not possess a firm basis for the rational assessment of myth.

We have already noted that most varieties of structuralism notoriously lack a theory of the competent social performer. Levi-Strauss is no exception as he fails to examine how myths are produced and reproduced over time. Not only does he often simply tear out a myth, isolating it from its context, but further, he overlooks how, in daily life, the social actor participates in the production and modification of myth. In this he shares a fault common to much structuralist thought: the lack of skilled, knowledgeable, human agency. We have already seen that the gap is evident in Saussure's *langue* and *parole*. What is missing is practical consciousness, the reflexive monitoring of conduct, in other words, the competence of each individual.

Finally, by arguing that the explanations of practice provided by participants are only the surface manifestations of deeper cognitive structures (invisible and unknown to the participants), Levi-Strauss lays himself open to having the same charge applied to himself. His structuralism cannot – by the rules of its own game – reflect on its own origins and structures. What codes underlie his structuralism? And why should it not be regarded as the product of its own particular set of socio-cultural circumstances? Answers to these questions can only embarrass his brand of structuralism.

Levi-Strauss' theory and method are idiosyncratic. Ambiguity characterises his writing which, though formidably argued, often reads more like a work of the imagination than a scholarly investigation. His own claim that *Mythology* can itself be read as myth is unlikely to endear him to empirical anthropologists or to enhance his credibility in their eyes. He frequently stands accused of failure to address himself to the problem of securing or anchoring an interpretation. His work, like Saussure's, is plagued by the problem of reference. These are telling criticisms, but it is possible that the imaginative power and ambiguity of his work are part of his appeal as he addresses himself to questions that are deep-rooted in the human psyche. Whatever its defects, there is no denying its bold address to fundamental problems, and we should welcome imaginative practices in the study of humanity.

Much of the above discussion and criticism of Levi-Strauss may seem far removed from the practice and preoccupations of teachers. What have the myths of the Bororo Indians to do with 4F on a wet Friday afternoon? Or binary oppositions with curriculum construction? Whilst I share the scepticism of many of his critics, I feel strongly that it would be inappropriate and short-sighted to dismiss Levi-Strauss as irrelevant to an understanding of schooling and education. His structuralism takes an extreme, unfamiliar form, but it contains potentially fruitful methods of fresh insights into educational theory and practice. His notion that we can 'read out' structures of mind from daily, conventional events is at once challenging, difficult and illuminating.

Moreover, although his stress on binary oppositions appears an oversimplification, a full appreciation of the nature–culture contrast, the paradoxes inherent in that contrast, and the mediations which go some way to resolving the paradoxes, can shed new light on aspects of schooling. The vocabulary of teachers (and parents) resonates with the expression 'it's (only) natural', but schools are particularly and peculiarly *cultural* institutions embodying paradoxes and contradictions. Whether and how those contradictions are *felt*, *experienced* by teachers and pupils are urgent matters for investigation, as are the resolutions they seek to reduce such tensions. In particular, the oppositions implied in teacher/pupil, male/female, knowledge/feeling, success/failure demand fresh examination. Levi-Strauss' unusual, refreshing and provocative views on such an everyday matter as the preparation and consumption of food can provide the stimulus for imaginative re-interpretations of schooling. The concept of transformation, for example, has received very little attention in English educational thought. To employ the concept directly in discussions of schooling would provide enlightening perspectives. What these approaches involve is Levi-Strauss' own conjunction of the very concrete with the very abstract: a procedure which presents a particular and uncomfortable challenge for all British teachers whose common sense is firmly rooted in the empirical tradition.

Levi-Strauss' *imagination* might help transform – or at least lighten and enlighten the study of education. Too many texts on education are banal and dull. Whatever else we may say about Levi-Strauss, his writing never has those characteristics. His work is an invitation to teachers to speculate, to imagine, to hypothesise about their work in a manner which breaks free of conventional, constraining categories – and in ways that are rarely found in the (ironically named) 'literature of education'. Although he is plagued by the problem of reference (how do we know whether his analyses are true or false?), there is an implied openness and flexibility about his interpretations which, for me, more nearly catch the complexity and richness of human thought and feeling than more matter-of-fact, unimaginative, narrowly pragmatic or scientific examinations of education. British teachers who read Levi-Strauss will become acutely aware of a style of thought which twenty miles of water have severed almost completely from their experience. But they will certainly find concepts which can throw fresh light on their own endeavour to understand and develop structures of thought.

NOTES

1   To say that most teachers are structuralists is a little like M. Jourdain in *Le Bourgeois Gentilhomme* who, when told of the distinction between poetry and prose, exclaimed with pleasure, 'For more than forty years I have been speaking prose without knowing it!' Nonetheless, I am quite serious in my assertion. Piaget's work has been a major force in all teacher preparation in the Western world and his views on structures of mind (however understood by teachers) exert a profound influence on educational practice. A valuable three-fold distinction to bear in mind is that of self-avowed structuralists; those writers who consciously employ *some* structuralist characteristics; and others who simply use the word 'structure' unselfconsciously as a useful term.

2   The best introduction to *Gestalt* psychology is still Max Wertheimer (1961). (Chapters 1–6 make particularly interesting reading.)

3 Magee (1978, pp. 205–6). The book of a splendidly heartening series which shows television at its educational best.

4 Magee (1978, pp. 213–14).

5 Gellner (1974, p. 99). Ernest Gellner is probably the most readable sociologist critic of structuralism.

6 Hirst (1975).

7 Piaget (1971). For the range and variety of Piaget's work *see*, for example, Mogdil, Johan and Celia (1976): 'estimated . . . eighteen thousand printed pages (the equivalent of seventy-five two hundred and fifty page books!)' (p. 17).

8 Piaget (1971, p. 4).

9 Piaget (1971, p. 62).

10 By 'Romantic theories', I refer to that long line of thought and feeling about children which includes such diverse figures as Rousseau, Wordsworth, Froebel, Pestalozzi and Susan Isaacs. It is characterised by emphasis on 'natural development', 'play', 'discovery', 'activity' and so on, and finds expression in many British infant schools.

11 Piaget (1971, p. 66).

12 There is no substitute for reading Piaget himself, although he is a difficult writer. For teachers, probably his most accessible and interesting book is *The Child's Conception of the World*, first published in English in 1929 and available also in paperback (1976). Two excellent introductions to Piaget (with critical commentaries) are Donaldson (1978) and Boden (1979).

13 Donaldson (1978, p. 133).

14 Piaget (1971, p. 63).

15 Lawton (1981, p. 52).

16 Cowan (1978).

17 Boden (1979, p. 152).

18 For criticism of Piaget's optimistic view of adolescent thinking see Peel (1968).

19 Levi-Strauss (1963).

20 The three stages of Levi-Strauss' work are best seen in:

   (a) (on kinship) *Elementary Structures of Kinship*, 1969 (very technical, much criticised).

   (b) (on classification) *The Savage Mind*, 1966 (possibly his best book).

   (c) (on myth) The four volumes of his *Mythology*, all translated by John and Doreen Weightman:

       1 *The Raw and the Cooked*, 1970.

       2 *From Honey to Ashes*, 1973.

       3 *The Origins of Table Manners*, 1978.

       4 *The Naked Man*, 1981.

   His ideas and methods are contained in the two volumes of *Structural Anthropology*, 1968 and 1977. *Mythology* and *Structural Anthropology* are difficult and often bewildering and frustrating books for anyone brought up in the Anglo-Saxon empirical tradition. (Names of publishers will be found in the Bibliography, pages 159–60.)

A highly readable, though critical, introduction is Leach (1970).

21 Music provides Levi-Strauss with a powerful analogy. Non-linear in form, it is a model for the deep structures of mind. Myths, to use Saussurian terminology, are *syntagmatic*: *parole*, linear, narrative, content. We grasp their realisation and meaning from those *associative* (paradigmatic) relations which are culture, *langue*, form. The structures of our mind enable us to create and interpret what we hear.

22 Levi-Strauss (1968, p. 216). Reported in Leach (1970, p. 65).

23 Leach (1970, p. 80).

24 Piaget clearly approves of Levi-Strauss. For an assessment which is far less appreciative, see Clarke (1981).

4 Structures of Society

How would you explain what is going on in a classroom or a school? What would be the prime focus of your attention, the important concepts and factors which most powerfully identify and influence action? In the previous chapter the focus was on structures of mind. In this we must discuss social structures and in Chapter 5, structures of feeling. What links all three structuralist approaches is the concern with structures, systems, wholes – rather than with individuals.

We have seen that Levi-Strauss' structuralism asserts the superiority of system over individual by according primacy to the unconscious structure of mind. It is these mental structures which determine all forms of cultural activity; they are society's 'reasons of which its members know little'. Such universal thought structures, claims Levi-Strauss, most powerfully explain human affairs. Other structuralist explanations, however, locate quite different mechanisms that underpin and impel social action. These are not structures of mind but structures of society or structures of social organisation.

When structuralism is concerned with the identification of the structures, patterns, systems and institutions of social life, then a very unlikely and heterogeneous collection of thinkers can be labelled structuralists (see note 1, Chapter 3, page 44). Thus, in its very broadest sense, such diverse social thinkers as Marx, Durkheim and Talcott Parsons could be viewed as structuralists (a description they would probably all have rejected even though 'structure' is central to their work). Each sought the material, organisational and ideological social imperatives of domination, coordination and normative order. Economic factors, social classes, fundamental modes of social relationships and institutions of society take precedence for them over structures of mind. Marx's well-known aphorism, 'It is not consciousness that determines being, but being that determines consciousness', makes quite clear his belief that the social and material conditions of life ('being') determine our thought, our view of the world ('consciousness'). In addition, Marx's emphasis on the centrality of history, and Durkheim's and Parsons' notion of 'function', radically divorce them from the structuralism of Levi-Strauss or Saussure who sought for the deep structures of mind and language.

Piaget's own preference for structures of mind is evident, and it is this which enables him to call Levi-Strauss an 'authentic' structuralist. For Piaget, Durkheim is simply a 'global' structuralist because he is concerned with social wholes: with groups and sub-groups. These totalities for Durkheim are primary explanatory concepts. For Piaget, 'authentic' (or analytic) structuralists seek the deep structures of mind which will explain such social wholes. Such deep structures 'are ultimately logico-mathematical models of observed social relations' invisible to participants, providing the transformation laws of society, whereas Piaget points out with an almost audible sniff: 'in Anglo-Saxon countries, the concept of structure tends to be reserved for observable relations and interactions'. He judges that Parsons 'goes beyond this too modest empiricism' as his structures are set out at a formal level approaching the degree of abstraction favoured by structuralists (anyone who has struggled with Parsons' writing will readily agree). Marx is placed by Piaget about halfway between global and authentic structuralism.

For teachers, this somewhat severe introduction may seem at first sight dauntingly distant from their own concerns and activities. Let me attempt briefly to establish some connections. To speak of 'the classroom', 'the school', 'the teacher', 'the pupil', 'the Local Education Authority', 'the parents' is to acknowledge the presence and force of social structure. So, too, do expressions like 'working-class pupils' or 'middle-class pupils' or 'middle-class values'. All are social categories or groupings that exist within other structures which themselves are social structures. These social structures ('the school', 'social class'), or structural elements ('the pupil'), powerfully influence the unique individuals who exist within and through them.

When four-year-old John enters his nursery class, or when sixteen-year-old Mary walks through the gates of her comprehensive school, those social structures that are 'classroom', 'school', 'education system', 'social class', 'society' will be at once their constrainers and their enablers, their shapers and resources for action. They are significant areas in which John's and Mary's identities, significances, beliefs and beings are formed. Both are 'pupils', and that everyday, taken-for-granted label is the social bedrock of their relationship with the adults they encounter. Those adults themselves are 'teachers', a social category which shapes *their* behaviour, beliefs, expectations. To lose sight of the way in which these *social* structures affect individual behaviour is to overlook very significant realities – and to miss seeing how change can occur. When John settles down to sorting coloured shapes and Mary to working out the area of a parallelogram; when John is praised for his effort and Mary rebuked for inattention; or when John listens to his teacher telling the story of Rapunzel or Mary writes her essay on the origins of World War I, these are not natural activities, they are *social*, and they are the consequence of those social structures: classroom, school, social class, society. Their activities are at once the process and outcome of being pupils. The social structures within which John and Mary have their being can be seen from the structuralist perspective as 'wholes' with their own *self-regulating mechanisms* and laws of *transformation* (schooling is most crucially engaged in the transformation of its members). Although John and Mary are unique individuals, their individualism from moment to moment (*synchronically*) is tempered by, realised through, defined in, their *relationships* within the social system that is education. In this, the gloomy structuralist consequence, *decentring of the subject*, can be glimpsed, as John and Mary are displaced as the focus of attention by their structural characteristics.

Fuller exploration of this structuralist approach to education must be deferred to later chapters. Here I will merely observe that most of what has been written in the sociology of education over the past two or three decades can be seen to be concerned with structure at two levels: society (macro) or school and classroom (micro). Thus, at the macro-level, sociology traditionally – whether orthodox (positivistic) or Marxist – has addressed itself to the relationships of education and society (e.g. Halsey, Floud and Anderson, 1961; Karabel and Halsey, 1977; Dale *et al.*, 1976). Here, the structure which has dominated explanations of schooling has been social class: a wealth of evidence testifies to class as the major focus of attention. The accumulated data on the relationship between social class and educational achievement contains an unequivocal message: the lower the class, the lower the attainment. Similarly, most explanations of the root causes of that clear pattern assert the grip of the class system ('capitalism' becomes a structural 'whole') over the influential elements: language, attitudes, child rearing practices and so on. Even those explanations which focus on the school rather than on home or community (e.g. grouping practices, curriculum, values) also have a marked tendency to reduce to 'the school as a middle-class institution'. The growth in recent years of structural explanations in terms of sex or race has not decreased the preoccupation with social class structures. The sad consequence of such structuralism has all too often been the too-casual equation that 'working-class' (or 'black' or 'female') equals 'failure' and causes that 'failure'.

At the micro-level there has been preoccupation with the school as an organisation and as a social system. The growing attention to classroom processes (and, less so, structures) is inspired by social theories which see men and women actively constructing their realities (e.g. Hammersley and Woods, 1976; Woods and Hammersley, 1977). At classroom level there is a sense in which *sociometry* could be seen as a structuralist enterprise, concerned as it is to map the informal or friendship relations of children. But my own view of both the theory and practice of sociometry in education (Evans, 1962; Gronlund, 1959; Hargreaves, 1967; Ball, 1981) is that the potential power of structuralist concepts has been very much neglected.

This division into macro and micro approaches to social structure is crude but not without its truth. It should be noted that some writers (with Marxists prominent) have striven to incorporate directly both levels into their work – in very different ways (e.g. Willis, 1977; Sharp and Green, 1975; Barton and Walker, 1981). There have been few examples of writers on education employing the type of structuralist thought as exemplified in Chapters 1 and 2. Bernstein is the only notable exception and his contribution will be examined in Chapter 7. In this chapter we must examine the work of two major writers who have attempted to bring structuralist concepts into conjunction with the analysis of social structures: Kurt Lewin and Louis Althusser. Lewin is the source of much research on group dynamics (that is, the micro-level); Althusser has worked at the macro-level, attempting to 'translate' Marxism into structuralism.

Lewin was a pupil of the *Gestalt* psychologist Kohler (see Chapter 3, page 30). His endeavour was to conceive social relationships as *Gestalts*, wholes, or, in his own term, as 'fields'. For him, each individual was situated in a 'total field': his social-psychological environment. He is unequivocal in his commitment to the structuralist notion of 'wholes':

The behaviour of a person or group is due to the distribution of forces
in the social situation as a whole rather than to intrinsic properties of
the individual.

The dynamics of the environment are engendered by *valency* (the
reciprocal relations of individual needs and the 'demand value' of
anything in the environment), and *accessibility* (the material and
psychological barriers in the total field). The concepts fields,
valency, accessibility, denote the origin in physics of Lewin's
model, and he attempted to develop a *psychological topology*, a
method of analysing the total field through topological geometry.
Lewin's mapping of the forces of the life space, the psychological
environment, through 'movements', 'paths', 'vectors' (again note
the origin in physical science of the terms) has had a tremendous
influence on the development of social psychology in which
network structures hold a central place.

Almost all teachers will be familiar with some of the work of
Lewin's pupils, Lippitt and White, whose study of leadership
styles (authoritarian, laissez-faire, democratic) and group dynamics has become one of the classics of teacher education (a
'classic', I must add, which is frequently misunderstood and much
in need of scepticism). Piaget has a very generous estimation of the
study of group dynamics ('a handsome example of analytic structuralism') and all teachers can profit from attention to it. For
example, Turner (1983) shows clearly that the structures and
processes of schools and classrooms have great influence on pupils'
learning. The contribution of teachers to, and their degree of
control over, these structures and processes, require the closest
study to enable effective change to occur, as (for example) the
wealth of school evidence testifying to the social benefits of
destreaming shows.

It is not only Lewin and the group dynamic theorists who
remind us that if you wish to change a person, you need to change
his whole situation. Karl Marx had grasped this principle many
years before and his notion of the 'whole situation' went much
deeper. Too often, a valid criticism of studies which concentrate
on the structures of the classroom or peer-group is that they lose
sight of the other structures, social and historical, within which
classrooms and peer-groups are embedded. To the relations of
structuralism with these macro structures we must now turn.

It is the ill-starred Louis Althusser,[1] in his efforts to accommodate structuralism to Marxism, who is the most significant figure
of recent years. His writing is a clear attempt to reformulate

Marxism in structuralist terms. To most teachers he is unknown, but he deserves to be much more widely studied, both for his structuralism and his belief that the education system is more important than family, church, mass media, law, politics, the arts, or sport in the maintenance and reproduction of society.[2]

Althusser's work is best seen as a major strand in the long and continuing debate between orthodox Marxism (emphasising the sacredness of Marx's texts) and revisionism (which attempts to re-write and re-interpret Marx in the light of modern conditions). The work of the Frankfurt School,[3] for example, is clear evidence of this debate in its efforts to substitute a revised version of Marx's writings for earlier, received, views. Althusser is not a member of the Frankfurt School, and rejects the label 'revisionist', but there is no doubt that, in spite of his claim to be 'orthodox', his work, like that of his contemporary Lacan, represents a very substantial departure from orthodox Marxism. Under the guise of claiming the rediscovery of Marx's original meanings, his work is a substantial rewriting of classical Marxism. For Althusser, this revision is much influenced by structuralism and his approach may appropriately be called structural Marxism.

Althusser's work has two major strands. First, it is a reaction against the classic Marxist notion that the economic structure is always the prime cause of social change. Second, it is a reaction against attempts to 'humanise' Marx, whether by those theorists who linked Marxism with Christianity, such as McIntyre (1969), or by those who place man ('the human subject') at the centre of explanation, particularly the phenomenologists and existentialists (e.g. Sartre and Merleau-Ponty). Althusser thus wishes to dispute both crude economic determinism and a humanistic Marxism. His ideas can therefore be discussed as, first, a critique of economism, and second, a critique of humanism.

Critique of Economism

Orthodox Marxism holds that material conditions of life, that is, economic conditions, determine all things.[4] To use Marxist terminology: the base governs the superstructure. This materialist/ economic view of history and society asserts that ideology – beliefs, ideas – arises from material conditions; that politics, religion, education are all subject to, and determined by economic relationships. Thus, to understand society is to understand its economic determinancy. Althusser reacts against such simple economic determinism and develops a much more elaborate theory of the role of material factors in social change. For him, the reliance on a purely economic interpretation of history is mistaken. To rectify Marxist theorising he employs three concepts: 'social formation', 'overdetermination' and 'structural causality'. In all three the influence of structuralist thought is very evident.

Social formation, he claims, is a concept that has more precision and more analytic power than the looser term 'society'. It is a 'totality' with three levels, ideological, political, economic, and Althusser argues that it is improper to assume causal relations between the three. Their relationships vary greatly between societies – for example, in capitalism or feudalism or in Asiatic modes of production. Any one of the three can be relatively autonomous, enjoying an independence that orthodox Marxism does not permit. This explanatory scheme may look merely like a 'combination of elements' approach, but Althusser's structuralism insists that he is not lapsing into causal pluralism or into eclecticism. Rather, asserting that he is giving a 'true reading' of Marx, he distinguishes two influences in the relations between the levels in any given social formation: the *dominant* and the *determinate*. Thus, in feudal society, the dominant structures were the political and ideological: a fusion of political power and ideological control evidenced in fealty and obligation. In capitalism, in contrast, the economic level is dominant in social affairs, having the more far-reaching influence as capital accumulation becomes more crucial. What Althusser is saying is that it is a mistake of Marxists to assert that 'economism' was dominant throughout history. Only in capitalism has it become dominant. And even there it is determinate only 'in the last instance', and as Althusser admits 'the lonely hour of the "last instance" never comes'. Such a qualified attitude towards the relationship of economics with other social elements reminds us forcibly of Engel's own strong denial that the economic element is the only determining element in history.[5]

In Althusser's concept of 'social formation' we see the structuralist notion of *wholeness*. It is a structure characterised by tension relations between its elements. In this social web, the economic relationships between man and man, group and group, are important (and in the (non-existent) last instance, determinate), but they are not *always* dominant. Ideological and political structures have substantial degrees of independence. Here the structuralist concept of *relationships* is very evident, as too is the notion of *transformation*, for the dialectic of change underpins Althusser's thinking.

For education the important consequence of Althusser's concept is to allow educational practice a much higher degree of independence from economic factors than many Marxist writers (e.g. Bowles and Gintis) are willing to permit. Indeed, as we have noted above, he accords tremendous importance to the education system. Although he inelegantly defines schools as 'Ideological State Apparatuses' (ISAs) the totality of his writing acknowledges the school's power and relative autonomy. In a striking analogy with music (an analogy incidentally that is almost a hallmark of structuralism – see the comment on Levi-Strauss in Chapter 3, page 39, and note 21, page 46) he makes that power manifest:

> All ideological State apparatuses whatever they are contribute to the same result: the reproduction of relations of production . . . the political apparatus by subjecting individuals to the . . . 'democratic' ideology . . . The communications apparatus by cramming every citizen with daily doses of nationalism, chauvinism, liberalism, moralism, etc., by means of the press, the radio and television. The same goes for the cultural apparatus (the role of sport in chauvinism is of the first importance), etc. The religious apparatus by recalling in sermons and the other great ceremonies of birth, marriage and death that man is only ashes unless he loves his neighbour to the extent of turning the other cheek to whoever strikes first. The family apparatus . . . but there is no need to go on. *This concert is dominated by a single score* . . . the score of the ideology of the current ruling class which *integrates into its music* the great themes of the humanism of the great forefathers . . . Nevertheless, *in this concert*, one ideological State apparatus certainly has the dominant role, *although hardly anyone lends an ear to its music*: it is so silent! It is the school.[6]

The second concept, *overdetermination*, is Althusser's key to explaining social change. He borrows the term from Freudian psychoanalysis: the idea that a neurotic effect can be achieved by different combinations of causes. Thus, there is no single cause, but, rather, multiple paths to the event. Althusser argues that the same overdetermination applies to historical change. Simple determinism is quite inadequate. The detailed explanation of an individual event must envisage it as the conjuncture of a variety of movements, of contradictions, which led up to it. The unique event is not determined, but rather overdetermined. Althusser cites in support Lenin's view of the Russian Revolution as an event not prompted by a single cause, but a particular combination of circumstances: the contradictions in the uneven development of society (a capitalist core amidst feudal relations); the uneven linkages with other capitalist nations (the weakest link in the chain of capitalism); the ravages of war, and so on. Piaget sees such overdetermination as the sociological counterpart of certain forms of causality in physics, and as such it is a transformational system which can replace traditional Marxist analysis. Overdetermination thus becomes not the resolution of contradiction but 'a necessary consequence of the inseparability of interactions'.

It is clear that overdetermination can be a powerful concept in the study of educational change at classroom, school and system level. The structuralist stress on *relationships* and on transformation, both embodied in the notion of overdetermination, can provide powerful insights into schooling. All education is over-determined: working-class underachievement, the development of comprehensives, the curriculum of a particular school, demands for school accountability; all have complex structural explanations.

Althusser's third concept, *structural causality* (or metonymic causality), gives primacy to the notion of overdetermination. It is very recognisably structuralist in its claim that the existence of structure is evident in particular events. Here are the Saussurian notions of *langue* and *parole*, absence and presence, transferred to the explanation of social affairs. Structural causality asserts that there is nothing *outside* the social system causing events; rather, it is the *whole* that is the social formation through the relationships of its structures, which determines action, and is evidenced in actions and events. This (although Althusser rejects the comparison) is somewhat like the Hegelian concept of 'expressive' causality, in which unique individuals or actions are expressions of a greater whole, representing in their individuality the 'essence' of that whole ('essences' are anathema to structuralists and Marxists alike, the former rejecting the notion in favour of 'relationships', the latter in favour of the concrete, material, 'real' world). The whole/part relationships of Althusser's model are like the whole/part relationships of Saussure: the absent whole (structure/*langue*) is present in the event (*parole*). Althusser uses 'effect' for 'event' and writes:

> . . . the effects are not outside the structure, are not a pre-existing object, element or space in which the structure arrives to *imprint its mark*: on the contrary, it implies that the structure is immanent in its effects, a cause immanent in its effect in the Spinozist sense of the

term, that *the whole existence of the structure consists of its effects*, in short
that the structure, which is merely a specific combination of its
particular elements, is nothing outside its effects.[7]

Here, albeit in an abstract, difficult form, is the clearest structuralist claim that the behaviour of pupils *embodies* those structures of
school and society in which they, the pupils, are *embedded*. John
and Mary *in* school, *are* school, *are* society; their every action
represents those 'absent' structures. This notion of structural
causality has powerful implications for education. It is my claim
(see Chapter 8) that we can thus 'read out' social structures from
everyday classroom events.

Althusser then, in his critique of Marxist theory, seeks to loosen
the grip of economic causation, to liberalise Marxist interpretations of history. For him the formula 'class relations producing
revolution' is neither sufficient nor adequate explanation because
it emphasises only *one* cause. Events are overdetermined, economic pressures are not always the most important cause. We can
thus draw on Althusser to reject simplistic social class explanations of schooling. Like Freud, his view of wholes or totalities is
that they are not harmonious or organic, but are tension systems.
It is the ever-present dynamic, indeed conflict, between structures
that explains events. The application of these concepts to education is powerful and relevant. To conceive of schools as tension
systems, as wholes, but not unified, consensual wholes, is to
perceive their realities more clearly.

But Althusser's critique of economism is not without its problems. Whilst his theory admirably counters crude material determinism, and offers valuable insight into the social and educational
system, nonetheless it has been strongly criticised for misapprop-
riation of Freudian over-determination; for its failure to explain
how structural causality actually represents causal relations between structure and event; for the obscurity of its 'last instance'
economic determinism; and for its comparative neglect of the
dominance of ideology in certain contexts.[8] His stress on the
importance and relative independence of education is welcome,
but his Marxism renders his analysis unacceptable for many
teachers.

Critique of Humanism

In Althusser's critique of humanism, the similarities with Saussure's thought are strikingly evident as he decentres man, reducing the human subject to a mere 'bearer' or 'supporter' of structure. In the relationship between individual and society, that vitally human term 'I', is to be understood only in terms of the social whole. Just as Saussure shows that a word has meaning only in the context of the totality that is *langue*, so too the individual exists in, and is given meaning and significance by, his relationships within social wholes, social formations. The focus for explanation for Althusser must be upon the social whole, not on the subject, 'I'. Thus, subjectivity is to be thought of in similar fashion to the embeddedness of 'the sign in the language'. Just as Saussure argued language had no positive terms, that words on their own had no significance, that only *langue* gives meaning to *parole*, so too Althusser argues that 'I', consciousness, the individual, are not given, but are constructed by and through the totality that is society. John and Mary become merely puppets, manipulated by, and images of, school, class, society. They are explained by the system.

Althusser takes issue with those humanist Marxists (Sartre, Merleau-Ponty, and members of the Frankfurt School) who assert 'the primacy of the human subject'. Such writers do not see the need for the human subject to be decentred in social analysis. Rather, they wish to put him or her at the centre of affairs: conscious, self-aware, active and, above all, *determining*. So too do most teachers: John and Mary are crucial factors in any explanation. Such humanism will not do for Althusser – not because of crude Marxist economic determinism, but because of structuralism (as the Saussurian analogy just given shows). He identifies these humanistic claims with political theories and with bourgeois politics: theories and practices that stress the individual and the rights of man. Althusser claims that such views are no more than the taking over of Marxism by the French bourgeoisie, and he saw his role as providing the French Communist Party with a more sophisticated critique it could use to mount an offensive upon such humanism.

Althusser's much criticised structuralist proposal is that individuals are no more than 'tragers' ('bearers' or 'supports') of the mode of production which is characteristic of the social formation in which they live. Men and women are 'bearers' of structures and these structures determine their individuality. Thus he treats man in terms of his incorporation in modes of production: for all his criticism of economism, Althusser is unable to break free of materialist explanation. As Giddens points out, such a view reduces human beings to 'structural dopes' of 'stunning mediocrity'. His true subjects are the 'places and functions' that agents occupy. John and Mary in their classrooms are to be seen primarily as 'pupils' – and, moreover, as pupils in a capitalist state where schools function to maintain exploitation.

The result of such a structuralist viewpoint is clearly seen in Rachel Sharp's interpretation of events in an English comprehensive school:

> What indeed was going on at Beachside Comprehensive was the reproduction of labour power in a docile form to meet the economic, political and ideological requirements of a capitalist system based on exploitation.[9]

Here, 'pupils' have indeed become 'bearers'.

Althusser's theory of ideology is crucial here, for ideology, he argues 'is indispensable . . . to shape men, to transform them'. He is therefore concerned to criticise the orthodox Marxist notion of ideology which sees it as false consciousness or as distorted communication. Marxists who so argue, he asserts, have got their Marxism wrong. Rather, he argues that ideology should not be seen just as a series of organised and systematic beliefs, or as the political views of a dominant group, but in a much broader way. As such it includes all those modes in which consciousness is formed, particularly in everyday life practices. Ideology, in this Althusserian version, is what acts on 'bearers' to transform them into human subjects. On these grounds he argues that the formation of subjectivity should be a central topic of study for Marxism. The study of ideology would be the study of the modes of everyday life in a society and the modes of practical action. Like anthropology it would concentrate on the daily habits, routines, taken for granted, ordinary elements of life. And such studies, he claims, would show fundamental ideological differences between capitalist societies and others. If this looks like some redress to his decentring of man, it is not, for he is certain that ideology is not man's conscious creation, but the mode through which consciousness exists. For all his emphasis on ideology as everyday life, Althusser has, as Giddens puts it:

. . . a blindness to the everyday fact that all social agents have an understanding, practical and discursive, of the conditions of their action . . . the involvement of actors' own purposive conduct with the rationalisation of action is lacking . . . as a consequence of his deterministic account of agency; hence the teleology of the system . . . supplants . . . that of the actors themselves.[10]

This precise identification of how Structural Marxism underestimates and undervalues the self-understanding and purposiveness of human beings shows once again the prime weakness of all structuralism: its neglect of (or incapacity to account for) human agency. A theory of the competent human actor is again seen to be noticeably absent. There is no acknowledgment of the knowledgeability and capability of individuals. The stress on structural determination, which sees John and Mary as 'bearers' of structure, fails to acknowledge the reciprocity of the relationship of individual and system. Human beings are not cultural or structural dopes, but Althusser's predilection for structures, like Levi-Strauss', misleads him into this dehumanising reduction. But his concern that ideology should be seen as familiar, mundane, taken-for-granted beliefs and practices is an important contribution which leads us directly to examine in Chapter 5 what I shall call 'structures of feeling'.

NOTES

1 The sad personal history of Louis Althusser is described in Karol (1980, pp. 93–5). From 1962 he was subject to periodic bouts of severe depression which eventually led to ever more frequent stays in psychiatric clinics. In the summer and autumn of 1980 he suffered a more serious depression than ever before and on 16 November killed his wife and was committed to a secure institution.

2 Althusser is a difficult writer and his ideas are uncongenial to many teachers. His view of education is put more technically than I have expressed it. He differentiates between what he calls *Repressive State Apparatuses* (government, administration, army, police, courts, prisons) and *Ideological State Apparatuses* (ISAs) (religion, education, family, law, politics, trade unions, communication, culture). His view is that:

> the ISA which has been installed in the dominant position in mature capitalist social formations . . . is the *educational ideological apparatus* . . . (it is) number one (Althusser, 1972, pp. 258–9).

3 Held (1982). The Frankfurt School is the name given to those

thinkers (e.g. Adorno, Horkheimer, Marcuse, Fromm, Lowenthal) associated with the Institute for Social Research established in Frankfurt in 1923. In the 1930s, with Hitler's rise to power, its members left for the United States. Some returned after the war. Its *critical theory* involved a rethinking of Marx and a questioning of positivism and instrumental reason (see Chapter 5, pages 83–4).

4   This economic determination is clearly expressed in Marx' Preface to the *Critique of Political Economy*:

> The mode of production of material life conditions the social, political and intellectual life processes in general. It is not the consciousness of man that determines their being, but, on the contrary, their social being that determines their consciousness.

(But see note 5.)

5   Engels, in a letter to Bloch in September 1890, much qualified orthodox Marxism's belief in total economic determination:

> According to the materialist conception of history, the *ultimately* determining element in history is the production and reproduction of real life. More than this neither Marx nor I have ever asserted (Krylov, 1976, p. 57).

6   Althusser (1972, pp. 259–60); my italics.

7   Althusser and Balibar (1970, pp. 188–9).

8   Giddens (1979, pp. 157–60).

9   Sharp *et al.* (1981, pp. 275–91).

10 Giddens (1979, p. 112).

5 Structures of Feeling

The best teacher taught us maths for a double period on Monday morning. He'd start off by saying 'Had a nice weekend everyone?' and he'd ask people what they'd done and sometimes we'd all fold up on the floor with laughter. He'd even come out with jokes himself. Then he'd say, 'Let's get on with some work, take your books out', and that was it . . . He was sociable. He just gave out the work and let you get on with it, and said 'Any trouble – come up and see me' . . . The way teachers start lessons is important. If the minute you get in there they shout at you, you think 'O, Christ, here we go.' If you go to talk to somebody and it's 'Oi, shut up!' that's when it all comes out, because it boils up inside you. You think 'Christ, he ain't going to rule me'.

I'd be walking down the corridor and one of the teachers would say 'Hey, Masefield.' Well, that's no way to treat you is it? It ain't as if they don't know your name 'cos you've been there long enough.[1]

The concept of structure of feeling is notoriously difficult to pin down. Its originator, Raymond Williams,[2] has spoken often of its elusiveness and defiance of easy definition. Yet there is no doubt of its existence or importance. The first teenager above who talks of his 'best teacher', the second who resents 'Hey, Masefield', both implicitly identify the feeling structure of their classroom or school encounter. In this chapter I shall make a number of attempts to approach, define and illustrate the notion of structure of feeling. In doing so, I shall, like Raymond Williams, remind the reader of its complexity, its heterogeneity, and of its pervasive influence on individuals. The length and the form of this chapter reflects and acknowledges the range, variety and significance of structures of feeling.

Structures of feeling are present in all social interaction, yet take many forms and can be analysed at different levels. To enter an infant classroom, watch a league football match, take part in a church service, travel in a foreign country, or be interviewed for a job is to be immediately aware of distinct but complex emotional and cultural climates. In each encounter we sense gross or subtle differences in affective tone, moral assumptions, beliefs. In each activity, feeling is central, informing, powerful, omnipresent. Our everyday experience, minute to minute, confirms the inescapability and press of feeling. Structures of feeling, however, do not refer to those directly experienced emotions such as anger, fear, eagerness, love and so on. Rather, they identify the particular modes and tones of relationship, perception and valuing which characterise any classroom, school or community (indeed, all forms of social grouping). They are the ethos or climate within which individuals have their being, and they are the values and assumptions which colour, influence, inform or dominate each individual's response. Whether we name or try to unravel their complexities in words such as ideology, beliefs, attitudes (or, less familiarly, *zeitgeist*, spirit), it is always clear that every individual moves within, embodies and expresses such affective states. These we can acknowledge as structures of feeling which are at once both local and general, personally experienced and yet characteristically social. They include systematic, coherent, well-known sets of belief (for example, Christianity, Marxism, Judaism); values (or, more accurately, value-complexes) such as individualism, democracy; and everyday, taken-for-granted assumptions about the world, variously referred to as 'common sense', 'obvious', 'familiar'. They are ways of seeing, interpreting and valuing the world: emotional states, dispositions of feeling, attitudes, which enable individuals both to 'see' reality and to evaluate it. They are judgments, explicit or implicit, on what is worth while and what is not, what should be and what should not be.

Thus my use of the term is much more relaxed than more formal notions of ideology or religious creed, for it encompasses those currents of feeling and belief which, whether precise or generalised, structure and pervade all human activity. The apparent generalities of the concept structures of feeling is not a weakness but rather an acknowledgment of the richness and plenitude of human conduct. It is at the same time a recognition that each example of social interaction requires interpretations which recognise the complex nature and sources of that diversity.

The source of the notion of structures of feeling is the work of Raymond Williams. Williams has for many years been a reference point for teachers from his analysis of education in *The Long Revolution* (1961). However, since that early examination of the relationships of culture and education he has given little direct attention to schooling. Nonetheless, in his criticism of literature and culture, and in his reworking of Marxism, are important concepts which can yield fresh insight into schooling. Of these, the most valuable is the concept of *structures of feeling*. His use of the term has expanded from its application to drama through literature in general to culture and society. His concern has always been to analyse the continuities from a particular literary work, through its particular form, to a general form, and thence to the relation of the form and the historical period.[3]

He argues that any institution (for him, drama; for us, schooling) takes its coloration, its character, its focus, its themes, from the community in which it is set: from the whole lived experience of that community, its material life, social organisation, ideas and beliefs. Williams' insistence on the *totality*, the essential interrelatedness of all that is lived and made in a particular community at a given time, marks out his structuralist endeavour. The artist draws on that totality, his individual work embodying and expressing the effect of a whole lived experience of his society. Williams' understanding of 'structures of feeling' is not that of well-formed, clearly set out, institutionalised beliefs: the ideologies of political parties or religions. Rather, his concern is with the everyday, taken-for-granted way of responding to a particular world, and he insists on direct experience, rather than formal argument or analysis as the mode of access to and acquisition of such structures of feeling. At once the most intangible, most difficult to define area of our lives, it is at once the most familiar: 'known primarily as deep *personal* feeling'. Such structures of feeling are indeed a structure, not random individual responses, but formations of commonly shared ways of seeing both ourselves and our world:

> We are talking about characteristic elements of impulse, restraint and tone; specifically affective elements of consciousness and relationships: not feeling against thought, but thought as felt and feeling as thought: practical consciousness of a present kind, in a living and interrelated continuity.[4]

Structures of feeling are for Williams cultural hypotheses, always related to the evidence of the arts and the society that is their context. The forms and conventions of art and literature are the indicators of such structures and the study of drama, poetry, or any artistic endeavour can reveal these structures of feeling, as attention progresses from local, particular, manifestations (*this* play, *this* poem) to those structures on which these unique manifestations draw, which they embody and express. The strength of Williams' work lies in the precise identification of certain historically connected structures of feeling in the work of particular dramatists and in his insistence on the need for scrupulously close examination of the complex relations between structure, forms, conventions and individual plays, novels or poems.

Williams' work is original and authoritative, but there are major ways in which my own use and interpretation of structures of feeling differs from his. First, in its application. Williams is concerned with literature, my own concern is to show the structures of feeling within schooling and their relation to structures outside the school. Second, my concern is not restricted, as is Williams, to *emergent* structures of feeling. He specifically rules out consideration of existing (*dominant* or *residual*) structures.[5] My own approach includes them, particularly those less formally organised, but nonetheless familiar, dominant, universal structures which bear customary labels: individualism, community, professionalism. Further, I wish to acknowledge, more I think than does Williams, the heterogeneity of structures of feeling: the presence of at least several significant structures detectable in any event. Finally, Williams' emphasis on practical consciousness, the assumptions of everyday life, of ways of seeing, he makes somewhat idiosyncratic and personal; the consciousness of a few gifted, even visionary individuals. My own preference is to emphasise that *all* people share these everyday perceptions. Whilst acknowledging that the geniuses he discusses (such as Ibsen, Strindberg, Chekhov) through their writing display acute insight into the feelings of their times and create the climate for the recognition of those feelings, my own view is that in everyday action, in particular in school life, teachers and pupils display, draw upon and reproduce, significant structures of feeling. My inclination is more towards Schutz' emphasis on the commonality of such experience[6] and on Giddens' insistence[7] on the competence and knowledgeability of everyone, rather than Williams' stress on individual writers or influential groups or classes. Williams' prime attention is on the artistic and the bourgeois levels of society, rather than on the structures of feeling experienced by *all* classes, *all* individuals. He reads structures out of 'great works'. My claim is that they are evident in daily life and in classrooms.

To grasp the sheer range of what is encompassed by the notion of structures of feeling which are common to all and which include both formal value systems and everyday taken-for-granted assumptions, let us consider two examples: the *Protestant ethic* and the *natural attitude*. Max Weber's *The Protestant Ethic and the Spirit of Capitalism*[8] examines the relationships between religious belief and economic life. Unlike Marx (who asserted that the latter determined the former), Weber's claim was that Protestant belief, in particular in its Calvinist version, produced modern capitalism. Thus, a structure of feeling had direct impact on material conditions and social interaction. Although Calvinists believed in predestination (that their fate after death was already determined by God), nonetheless they also believed that an indicator as to whether they were among the elect was success in work. Hard work and financial achievement signified a state of blessedness; success implied spiritual salvation. However, Calvinism also demanded asceticism and frugality: saving and reinvesting, not spending or squandering. Such self-discipline ensured capital accumulation as reinvestment in business produced further wealth. A belief system (one example of a structure of feeling) had powerful social and material results. Weber's Protestant ethic (however disputable) has become part of modern consciousness and the structure of feeling it represents has become formalised as a series of well-known indicators, such that the term at once calls up notions of the value of ambition, achievement, individual effort, deferred gratification. Its manifestation in schools is analysed below (pages 68–71).

In contrast we can note a development of Weber's work, the phenomenology of Alfred Schutz.[9] Here, instead of fairly clearly formulated beliefs ('the Protestant ethic', 'Marxism', 'Catholicism', and so on), the structure of feeling is variously referred to as 'the natural attitude', 'common sense', 'recipe knowledge' and represents the implicit presuppositions upon which formal beliefs and religions, and action itself, are based. Structures of feeling are seen as (to use the familiar expressions of the phenomenologists) 'everyday', 'taken for granted', 'unproblematic', 'subjective meaning', 'cookery book knowledge'. These beliefs represent ways of seeing the world which are taken as 'given', in the sense that they are obvious and unquestioned, and they comprise common-sense assumptions about both what is true and what is valuable. Hence, they constitute guides for action and are drawn upon unconsciously in every moment of social interaction. These stocks of common-sense knowledge are unexamined by participants in that they are not seen as open to theorising about (that could only be a task for a philosopher or social scientist, and it appears as at best a puzzling, and at worst a pointless, activity to those participants). This pragmatic or tacit knowledge (or 'practical consciousness' as Giddens calls it) is constantly used as a *resource* by all social actors. Although it is typically non-discursive (in the sense that few actors can formulate it – that is, give its rules or precisely specify the values or perceptions it embodies), it is not unconscious, merely taken for granted as obvious. There is a strong sense in which practical consciousness testifies to the competence of every individual, for it shows that every individual knows a great deal about the society of which he or she is a member. In Giddens' terms it is

> . . . tacit knowledge that is skilfully applied in the enactment of courses of conduct, but which the actor is not able to formulate discursively.[10]

It is important to recognise here that although I am speaking of 'knowledge', I assert that this knowledge is most essentially in the form of belief: it is a structure of feeling: a conflation of common-sense views on how the world *is* and *should be*.

These beliefs probably become most obvious in humour, when conventional assumptions about normality are breached, when expectations are not fulfilled, when something 'bizarre', 'exotic', 'strange', 'unfamiliar' occurs. When a pupil imitates a teacher for the amusement of his friends, much of the laughter derives from knowledge of the rules, the normalities, that are being disrupted.

The notion of structures of feeling allows us partially to dissolve the distinction between structure and event which structuralism implies. Thus, the notion of practical consciousness enables us to see that structure is instantiated *in* event; it is at once drawn upon and expressed by the individual actor: structure is simultaneously the medium and outcome of event. When the teacher says, 'Listen, dear' (or 'Listen Smith'), she evidences a structure of feeling which is both outside and inside her, which pre-exists and yet is created anew, which is at once the context of belief and emotional tone and the unique instance of it. To see social interaction in this way is to reconceptualise the traditional polarities of structure/event, social/individual, conscious/unconscious, general/particular, theory/action. That reconceptualisation is achieved through the acknowledgment of human competence.

The realities of everyday life towards which the work of Schutz directs us also acknowledges the existence of multiple realities. Structures of thought and structures of feeling can be identified behind and within any event to indicate how quickly and competently each individual moves between spheres of experience:

from the literal to the metaphysical, from sacred to profane, from scientific to poetic. These realities are recognised (and created) by practical consciousness and produce appropriate responses. What may appear as discrepant, disjunctive experiences are all too easily encompassed and absorbed by the individual resourcefully drawing on the appropriate structure to give meaning and relevance particular application. When Ronald King (1978) speaks of the multiple realities of the infant classroom he acknowledges the teachers' definition and creation of the reality of everyday life in those classrooms and their creation of other orders of reality, reading, story, number, which children learn to share and re-create.

Structures of Feeling in Schooling

What structures of feeling are evidenced in the everyday world of schools and classrooms? Every classroom *has* its distinctive ethos; that is certain. It is however much easier to *feel* it than *describe* it. What must now be attempted is to turn these feelings into words, albeit always with an uneasy sense of tension and provisionality which must accompany such an endeavour. Later in this chapter I shall examine a number of studies which bear witness to the range and variety of climate or ethos to be found. First, however, I shall argue that most of the elements identified are contained within three major structures, each one a complex web of tones, moods, dispositions and orientations, which represent distinctive and coherent structures of feeling. The three structures can be called *achievement*, *social welfare* and *spontaneity*. Their presence in schools and classrooms is evidence of their wider, social existence, as they are drawn upon and reproduced by, and in, teachers and pupils. Within themselves and between the three structures, are contradictions and conflicts which receive differing acknowledgment from participants. The 'official' view (that is, the teacher's view or what may be called the liberal ideology) assumes that the three structures *can* be reconciled, that it is the task of school to accommodate and harmonise them. In contrast, 'unofficial' views (whether Marxist, deschooling, or pupil perspectives) stress their incompatibility and irreconcilability, seeing the school as a site of conflict and struggle through opposing structures of feeling. A sketch of the three major structures reveals the tensions in and between them and will serve as a framework for discussion of particular investigations.

Achievement

The structure I have called *achievement* is at once obvious, pervasive and dominant. Its manifestations and influences are simultaneously overt and hidden, direct and subtly indirect, compelling
and seductively persuasive. Its elements and their various forms
and practices are richly heterogeneous. At its starkest, the feelings, values and beliefs it represents are concerned with the
importance of work, 'busyness', occupation, 'getting on', 'suc-
ceeding', effort. The teacher's 'get on with your work' is its most
obvious practice. Her setting of tasks in reading, writing, or
number, and her continuous, unrelenting assessment of the
pupils' attainment in these tasks is its sharpest, most persistent
manifestation. Achievement is, in school, essentially *individual*
achievement. If achievement is the major structure of feeling,
individualism is its core, for each pupil must come to terms with
his or her own personal success or failure in school work. From the
earliest days in school, from personal progress through the books
in a reading scheme, to the gradings of O-level or A-level examinations, each pupil learns that what inevitably matters in school,
what is valued, what counts as success, is the level of individual
achievement in school subjects. The steady, unremitting, corro-
sive (or, for some, confirming) process of individual assessment
makes clear the structure of feeling that is achievement. When, in
a well-known television series on a comprehensive school, the
caring, person-oriented headmaster exclaims, with evident joy,
'He's got 3 As!' as he discovers a pupil's A-level results, the feeling
structure is laid bare and the central value system of the school (all
schools) is sharply revealed. The concomitant of individual
achievement is *independence*: a concern for self-reliance, individual
responsibility and resourcefulness, in its most acute form a
Samuel Smiles' philosophy of self-help, of 'standing on your own
two feet'. The examination or testing procedures in any school
provides striking evidence of this structure of feeling in action. No
one who has participated in an examination can avoid experiencing the sharp realities, the beliefs given concrete expression, of the
achievement ethic. Each candidate sits alone, isolated, forbidden
to cooperate or converse with others, thrown entirely on his or her
own resources, forced to give an account by which personal
success or failure will be measured in percentages or literal grades
which will, thereafter, be permanent, objective recordings of
achievement levels. In the *process* of the examination can be seen
how this structure of feeling is drawn upon, expressed, revivified,

reproduced. Consciously or unconsciously, positively or negatively, it shapes the attitudes of participants; it is inescapable in schooling, permanently present. Sharply evident in examinations, it is no less powerful in the daily setting and assessing of tasks in all classrooms.

Some theorists take this structure of feeling to be one of the major malformations of capitalism; Marxists pinpoint it as a distortion of social and personal development. But such special condemnation is misplaced, for *achievement* is a central feature of all schooling irrespective of its ideological setting. The achievement ethic is prominent in *all* schools; it is a necessary consequence of any insistence of learning to read or write, of institutional study itself. Assessment of individual learning is a feature of all schools in all cultures. And in those schools which place high value on the cognitive aspects of the curriculum, which stream or set by ability, and which stress examination success, it is the prime feature.

Achievement, as a structure of feeling, is underpinned and legitimated by rationality. The success it demands in cognitive tasks is subject to precise measurement; and those tasks are set on reasoned grounds. The claims of schooling and its curricula arise not simply from traditional or arbitrary bases, but through rational appraisal of education, society and individual. The abundance of educational theory is testament to that fact. But to recognise this is to recognise that rationality itself is a structure of feeling: a belief that 'being reasonable' is not simply good counsel, but that it will produce, if not total accord, at least a high measure of consensus on what should be done. That such consensus does not exist (what *should* go on at William Tyndale?) speaks more to the existence and power of structures of feeling than to the value-freedom of rationality. What rationality insists upon – and what is evident in schooling – is order, discipline, restraint, caution, codification, classification, a concern for logicality and clarity, a distrust of ambiguity. Such characteristics are the hallmark of certain feeling states, and in different degree they are elements in the affective tone, the ethos, of classrooms.

At the individual level, achievement implies personal ambition, getting on, getting out of lower social status groups. It implies a concern not simply to be in control of one's own life but to have power and influence over others. Such ambition is, for teachers, built into the social structure of their own profession or occupation. The desire to climb the promotion ladder is testament to the achievement structure of feeling. Success is synonymous with promotion, for to remain a Scale 1 classroom teacher is deemed somehow improper, a failure. The apologetic tone of some excellent class teachers for their preference to remain where they are rather than to seek promotion to headships or higher scale post shows how the structure has bitten deep into the attitudes and views of those teachers. For the majority of teachers the structure of feeling is taken for granted. It is unproblematic, desirable, obvious. The thought that teaching could somehow *not* be about getting on, not gaining promotion, is neither entertained nor conceivable. The subtle yet powerful equation of merit, value, progress, even goodness, with numbers is as present in the daily experience of teachers (Scale 1 is inferior to Scale 4) as it is for pupils (Grade D is inferior to Grade A; 5 out of 10 is inferior to 9 out of 10). It is how the measure of attainment is subtly and malignantly transformed into a measure of personal and social worth that is the indicator of the strength of the structure of feeling.

For pupils the achievement ethic all too often transforms the hierarchy which inevitably results from the measurement of cognitive activity into a hierarchy of moral and social worth. Rational assessment of certain intellectual competences metamorphose into global labels of the 'good pupil'. Achievement in school learning necessarily produces graded subdivisions of pupils, whether as the now largely defunct class order list or as the less obvious teacher assessment or exam grade. Some pupils perform better at school subjects than others, and gradings or systems of streaming or setting, within classes or between classes, reveal and objectify that hierarchy. Such a hierarchy reveals another strand in the achievement structure of feeling: competition.

Teachers and pupils, like other members of society, are divided in their attitude towards competition. Is it healthy or unhealthy, effective or ineffective, worthwhile or insidious? What is clear is that the special feature of capitalist society is how its economic and social structures are underpinned by this very structure of feeling: competition, or a belief in 'market forces' as the measure of all things. In Mrs Thatcher's Britain or Mr Reagan's America, the dominance of a belief in the value of competing in the market place needs no argument or proof, it is self-evident. The equation of strength and value is complete. What is not so obvious, and what may be the distinguishing characteristic of education under capitalism, is that achievement involves and harnesses, draws on and develops the competitive spirit, the concern to do better than your neighbour. Individual success is at the expense of other individuals and the weakest goes to the wall. The rhetoric of competition argues, however, that education, like the economy, is not a zero-sum game, there is not a finite stock of knowledge or wealth available where one man's gain is another's loss. Rather there can be increases in the totals available. But, nonetheless, just as we are increasingly aware of the finitude of the world's physical resources available for development or exploitation, so too the expansive, optimistic view that academic success can be personal, non-competitive, or competitive only against the intrinsic demands of 'the subject itself', is permanently under attack.

First, it is under attack from those who see the world (and schooling) as essentially competitive and who struggle to assert their view. Second, it is under attack from the increasing impingement of economic constraints on opportunities and rewards available in and through education itself; there *are* scarce resources, and those will be unequally distributed depending on effort and achievement. The third attack we have already noted: the tendency to equate cognitive attainment with moral value; low achievers are less valuable or 'valued'. Such points emphasise the pressure of structural forces. The achievement structure of feeling which puts such heavy stress on competition acts as a massive counter-weight against the evident goodwill of those individuals who attempt to combat it. To argue this is not to engage in abstract assertions, for the signs are visible daily in the life of any school; the structure of feeling that is achievement is to be found in the formal curriculum, in the cognitive–intellectual subjects or tasks which predominate. The timetable itself represents the demand for effort, it signifies the value of achievement, symbolising systematic targets set for pupils. Achievement for all is the transparent aim; the structural consequence of failure for many is less remarked. Rather, achievement becomes a matter of relative achievement, of 'doing the best you can', with the lower evaluation of that 'best' underplayed. The curriculum makes clear what knowledge is valid and valuable; and assessment confirms its judgment (a CSE pass is not as valuable as GCE). In the same way that parity of esteem for modern and grammar schools proved a naive ideal, so too the elements of the achievement structure of feeling continue to ensure the very different valuation of the processes, curricula and outputs of the comprehensive school.

Social welfare

If achievement signifies the importance of *difference*, of hierarchy, of inequality, an equally obvious structure of feeling in every school stresses *similarity*, sharedness, equality, commonality. This I have called *social welfare*. Its surface structure is like achievement, for it attends to individuals; but its deep structure is concerned with feelings about shared characteristics and group well-being. The school indicators are 'pastoral care' and 'community'. The pastoral care system of any school, whatever its form, exemplifies this structure of feeling. Organised by 'House' or 'Year' or 'Tutor Group', the wholes such words represent embody the structuralist affirmative ideal. A sharp, if cynical, contrast can be made by viewing a school's pastoral care system as a curriculum casualty clearing station, repairing the damage inflicted by the insistence on achievement. The social welfare structure of feeling can be seen as contesting the major elements of achievement, for it stresses cooperation rather than competition, interdependence rather than independence, group solidarity rather than individual mobility.

The words 'caring' and 'concern' are central, and its rhetoric speaks of 'the whole child' rather than of a narrow interest in cognitive achievement. It echoes those structures and forces which created (and represent) the Welfare State, for its concern is not only with the successful but with the failures and the weak. It is self-consciously humanitarian in its concern for individual and group health; 'health' that is of all types: physical, emotional, spiritual, social. Because of the culture in which this structure of feeling is set (British, late twentieth-century) it is interpenetrated by, and infused with, individualism. Its focus on the 'unique child' and the 'development of each individual's full potential' is underpinned by very heterogeneous legitimations, from liberalism's notions of freedom, autonomy and individual privacy, to such diverse psychological theories as those of Piaget and Freud. This emphasis on the individual sets it apart from comparative examples of the social welfare ethic in Communist countries where the relation of individual to group is one of subordination. In its Western, particularly British, manifestation, the structure of feeling that is social welfare strives to accommodate and incorporate individualism into its emphasis on group well-being. That accommodation is necessarily uneasy, but the rhetoric of the structure of feeling seeks to dissolve such disjunctures; the welfare of the whole child and the welfare of the school are seen as synonymous, the qualities of compassion, tolerance, empathy, cooperation will result in individual *and* group health. But to identify these structures of feeling is to acknowledge that in pupils' experience of daily school life the feeling structures are in tension, often in direct opposition. The stress on individual achievement imposes demands which deny and thwart feelings of togetherness, belonging or sharing.

'Community' is another aspect of the social welfare structure of feeling. The wholesale redesignation of 'community schools'; the stress on positive relationships with 'the community' and the active involvement of schools and community; together with the concern *within* schools to 'build a community', to create 'we-feeling' amongst all its members, all these are indicators of the social welfare structure. They also reveal the difficulties of its relationships with achievement. 'Fitting-in' and 'getting-on' make awkward bedfellows. Teachers wish pupils to see their schools as good places to be, as friendly, warm, caring communities. Many schools are successful in creating that feeling in some of their pupils. Many are not, as truancy, boredom and indiscipline testify. The root of such failure lies much in the disparity which exists between the achievement and social welfare structures of feeling. The rhetoric to which teachers are committed all too easily blurs those disjunctions in its preference for illusory harmony. Pupils perceive the sharp opposition and substitute their own definitions of community as they perceive the school's achievement labels:

> Half of us were clever and half weren't. At first I wanted to be clever and I used to listen to the teacher: but as time went on I used to sit further to the back to be with my friends.[11]

Spontaneity

The two structures of feeling discussed above both appeal to rationality as their guiding principle and justification. The third structure of feeling is non-rational and can be seen as contesting both achievement and social welfare. I have called it *spontaneity* – or more simply 'fun'. It is primarily evident among pupils in their friendship groups. The gang seeking 'kicks' or the peer group 'having a laugh', are primarily concerned with enjoyment, hedonism, humour. The intuitive, immediate pleasure-seeking stands in sharp contrast to the stern demands of deferred gratification on which achievement insists. The protestant ethic of 'wait' and 'delay', of reserving pleasure until later, until work is complete, and then only tasting it cautiously, is almost irreconcilable with the immediate, present-oriented, enjoyment-seeking of spontaneous feeling. The order, control, rationality and organisation which are the characteristics of schooling's curricular and community activities are threatened by the anarchic expressivism of the 'fun' subculture.

In its most extreme manifestation certain hippy groups of the 1960s (in fact or in popular imagination) represent this structure of feeling: 'let it all hang out', 'don't think of the future', 'have it now'. Such extremes are past and discredited, but the structure of feeling is still present in many forms, from its institutionalised expression in the mass media and gambling to the easy hedonism of the peer group where friendship, luck and enjoyment are central assumptions. The daily experience of all teachers testifies to the existence and power of this third structure of feeling. Very seldom does any classroom teacher lose sight of the need to restrain, control and re-direct the spontaneous, pleasure-seeking, task-avoiding impulses of his/her pupils. In childhood itself, the human origins of the structure of feeling are clearly visible in the spontaneity of the young child. What the adult world, and schooling in particular, does is to channel, divert, restrain, control, and transform that spontaneity into legitimate and acceptable activities, whether as the work of the achievement ethic or the active concern of social welfare. In curriculum terms, sport, physical education, craft, expressive and aesthetic subjects represent formal controls on this structure of feeling: they harness the elemental self-centredness to useful, desirable and hence legitimate processes and outcomes. In the primary school, particularly in the progressive ideology, the oppositions of these basic structures are resolved or argued away, by making them not simply complementary but identical: 'play is the child's work', 'children learn best by following their own interests, through enjoyment'. But such resolutions mask crucial incompatibilities: the 'freedoms' that spontaneity seeks are not the 'freedoms' of achievement or social welfare.

The rhetoric of schooling – freedom, autonomy, self-development and fulfilment of potential – is common to all three structures, but the interpretations and realities of each are very different. Individual achievement, social welfare and spontaneous enjoyment make more for tension and conflict than for stability and harmony. But through clearer awareness of these structures and how they are present in their own schools and classrooms, teachers may reduce harmful conflict.

Studies of Schooling

We can see, in certain recent studies of schooling, some of the elements making up these three major structures of feeling. David Hargreaves' long study of secondary schools reveals certain value complexes which bear heavily upon pupils and teachers. His first book[12] showed vividly, in his identification of an anti-school, delinquescent group of pupils, that structure of feeling I have called *spontaneity*: the pursuit of immediate satisfaction, the rejection of school achievement and ambition, the overturning of conventional standards of courtesy, politeness, respect for property, wholesome recreation. Fifteen years later in *The Challenge for the Comprehensive School*[13] Hargreaves brings together his accumulated experience to rework the same theme but with different emphasis. In his address to the questions of what English comprehensive schools are like and could or should be like he is much concerned with feeling, with how feeling and belief issue in everyday experience, in the 'social relations of the encounter'. His diagnosis makes gloomy reading; the daily experience of school for many pupils is one of boredom and fear. Pupils find the school's stress on the cognitive–intellectual aspect of the curriculum both tedious and threatening. The major message they learn is that:

the only knowledge and skills which really count in school . . . are primarily intellectual–cognitive in content.[14]

Although teachers do not intend it, other areas of experience (aesthetic–artistic, affective–emotional, physical–manual, personal–social) are subordinated to cognitive–intellectual demands. The result is not simply to turn pupils off; rather Hargreaves interprets the boredom and fear of failure he sees as the result of a sustained assault on working-class dignity. The hierarchical social relations of the encounter of the classroom result in the destruction of dignity; the working-class pupil loses a sense of being worthy, of possessing creative, imaginative faculties and having power to effect personal or social change. As a consequence, argues Hargreaves (and here the link with and development of his earlier work becomes clear), a school counter-culture emerges, drawing on what resources there are to hand. Following Willis[15] he identifies the major resource as a segment of working-class values: trouble, smartness, fate, independence. It is by drawing on this structure of feeling (akin to spontaneity) that the determinism of schools and society – the drive to failure, to dead-end jobs – can be challenged, undermined and transformed by positive response. Thus Hargreaves defines youth culture (apparently negative, hedonistic, anarchic) as an attempt to recover a sense of community, of solidarity, which does not exist for them in school ('failures'), home (isolated, privatised), or work ('hands' on an assembly line). Clearly Hargreaves is here identifying the structure of feeling that is community. His endeavour is to restore that structure and its impulses to the centre of schooling by making community studies the core of his curriculum proposal, and by recovering a sense of loyalty, obligation and corporate spirit in shared festivals, performances and activities. But Hargreaves' book is best seen as an attack on individualism. It is this structure of feeling that he sees as being excessively present in the comprehensive school. For Hargreaves the aims of education have become excessively defined in terms of the *individuals* it should produce, rather than the *society* desired. This preoccupation with individualism, bolstered by the child-centredness of such thinkers as Piaget, Rousseau, Dewey and the meritocratic ideal, has resulted in scepticism and a practice which diminishes and destroys a sense of corporate identity, a sense of belonging. In the decline of school rituals, school uniform, the class or form group, Hargreaves sees not simply scepticism but cynicism: 'Up the School!' has utterly different resonances in 1982 from earlier decades. Teachers themselves are 'deeply involved with a *culture of individualism*',[16] he asserts, which threatens loyalty or esprit-de-corps. In the everyday life of the school he sees the 'Paddington Station effect' (bells ring, all change) and the 'Luton Airport effect' (the endless carrying of bags because there is no firm form room base). Hargreaves' solution is to replace 'the fallacy of individualism' with aims which will restore dignity by creating a sense of being valued *by*, and competent *in*, a social group. His enterprise is to 'rescue dignity from individual connotations'[17] and to acknowledge the school's key function as being 'to breathe life into the spirit of association'. As such it can be called a structuralist endeavour.

From Hargreaves' curriculum prescriptions we can turn to research into school accountability. The Cambridge Accountability Project, studying six comprehensive schools, revealed that certain structures of feeling underpinned accountability practices:

professionalism, individualism, community, democracy.[18] The complex heterogeneous feelings which each of these clusters of belief represent were evidenced in the actions and perspectives of the hundreds of teachers and parents at the six schools. *Professionalism*, a set of beliefs about relationships with others, clearly informed and influenced teachers' actions as they strove to accommodate notions of service to clients with assumptions about their autonomy and monopoly of practice. Most teachers appeared to have made a satisfactory resolution of the tensions implicit in believing simultaneously in their own professional autonomy and the need for public accountability. What was also clear was that parents felt a deep ambivalence in their attitude to teachers: on the one hand a trust in the teachers' competence (or, certainly, a belief that the teachers' job was to 'get on with teaching') and, on the other hand, a feeling of powerlessness because of what was seen as the lack of any real accountability. This ambivalence appeared to arise from that structure of feeling I have identified as professionalism.

The second structure of feeling, *individualism*, was equally powerful. Both teachers and parents drew on deeply held beliefs about *personal autonomy*: the right to determine one's own life, take one's own decisions. Thus 'independence', 'self-direction', 'getting-on' were much-used expressions. Then, too, the idea of *human dignity*, of the intrinsic worth of each individual was a key component of this structure of feeling. It was clearly evident in each school's aims, its pastoral care system, and in every parent's touchstone of the school's success: the criteria by which they measured accountability was how well the school provided for *their* son or daughter. Another component of individualism was also much in evidence: the right to privacy, which includes liberty of conscience, thought and feeling; freedom of opinion and freedom to live life in one's own way. Although a study of school practice would show many qualifications to the right of privacy, there is no doubt that in the beliefs and language of teachers and parents it is massively present ('tolerance', 'pluralism', 'make up your own mind', 'choose'). A further element of individualism – *self-development*, the unfolding of personal talents – was enshrined in the structure of teacher and parent beliefs: the expectation that schools should enable children to 'make the best of themselves'.

Community was the third structure of feeling identified in the accountability research. Notions of 'belonging', 'caring', 'concern' and 'commitment' were obviously and centrally as present in each of the six schools as they are in the wider culture. Almost all teachers saw themselves committed to the notion of 'the school *as* a community', and they were also evidently concerned for the school to serve the local community. Parents drew on the community structure of feeling in somewhat different ways; although they wished their children to 'fit in', to be happy, to get on with teachers and peers, they also frequently expressed concern about control, order and discipline. This latter emphasis contrasted strongly with the warm, organic, friendly relationships which 'community' often implies. Further, parents' notions of community were strongly future-oriented: the task of school was to prepare for work or higher or further education. One typical index of such concern was that the school should 'push the kids'. But whatever the specific manifestations or emphases of the *community* structure of feeling, their contrasts and tensions with *individualism* were clear and powerful.

The fourth structure of feeling revealed in the accountability research was *democracy*; the calling of 'rulers' to account, the belief that each individual has a right to participate in decisions which affect him/her. Such sentiments are inextricably and centrally part of English culture and are the source of accountability demands. The Project found that the relationships between school accountability and democracy are at once complex and uneasy, uncertain and tenuous. Any hint that democratic accountability might mean lay control of schools was anathema to teachers. Democratic structures of feeling were clearly subordinate to those of professionalism. The formal expression of this structure of feeling, the governing body of each school, was regarded with scepticism by most teachers and by a sense of uncertainty and constraint (or even powerlessness) by most governors themselves. But there nonetheless is no doubt that the structure of feeling that is democracy is at once a major influence on, and a major resource for, teachers and parents. It is drawn upon and applied with different force in different areas: curriculum, standards, staffing, discipline, finance, resources. It is a crucial source of ambivalence because schools themselves are *not* democratic (although they often figure as such in the rhetoric of education), and because the curious blend of trust and mistrust embodied in 'democracy' ('you can vote them out of office') applies very uneasily to schools staffed by full-time professionals committed to building relations of trust with pupils and parents. What the accountability research revealed was the existence and pervasiveness of structures of feeling and the complexity and interpretation of their relationships. They had powerful impact upon human action, and in subtle, varied and adaptive ways were drawn upon and expressed by parents and teachers and pupils as they moved within and created their social worlds. The structures bore with different weight on different people at different times, but they constituted the inescapable social, shared pressures which at once confront and exist within each unique individual.

Other research into secondary education reveal structures of feeling which can similarly be accommodated to the three-fold framework of achievement, social welfare and spontaneity. Gerald Grace has shown the complexity of the structures of feeling within which the nineteenth-century teacher was embedded and upon which he drew to fulfil his obligations:

> The basic imperative to control coexisted with a genuine humanitarian and Christian impulse to help, a radical interest in equipping the people for political membership, a capitalist interest in rendering them competent and efficient as workers, a religious interest in making them 'good', and a liberal/cultural interest in 'elevating' and 'refining' them to an appreciation of a higher order of culture'.[19]

He identifies specifically a 'Christian or missionary ideology' which helped sustain the Victorian teacher of working-class children. Such a structure of feeling was historically present then, but it would appear to have given place today to a secular version of social welfare: the impulse to help is still there but its manifestations and rhetoric have undergone tremendous changes over the century.

Paul Willis' well-known study[20] of 'how working-class kids get working-class jobs' approaches structures of feeling through a notion of *division*. He argues that working-class 'lads' reject the school (and its stress on *individualism*) because they live in a society which makes sharp evaluative distinction between mental and manual ('good with the head' better than 'good with the hands'), gender (male better than female), and race (white better than coloured). His claim is that, for all the school's 'degree of liberalism and formalistic equality', these fundamental divisions of feeling and valuing in both culture and institutions reproduce class society and its inequalities. His work is particularly relevant for its assertion that his 'lads' use certain elements of their working-class culture as a resource on which they draw to maintain their identity. Those elements represent a structure of feeling opposed to the achievement ethic of school: toughness, challenge to authority, excitement, luck, and a desire for freedom. Here again is the *spontaneity* structure of feeling contesting the demands of the cognitive–intellectual curriculum.

Stephen Ball's study[21] of a comprehensive school implementing a change to mixed ability grouping identified three 'group perspectives' among the teachers. Following Becker he sees these as:

> a coordinated set of ideas and actions a person uses in dealing with some problematic situation, to refer to a person's ordinary way of thinking about and feeling about and action in such a situation.[22]

These 'group perspectives' can be seen as structures of feeling. The three Ball identifies are *academic* (concerned with 'standards', excellence, the brighter child, the academic subject), *disciplinary* (concerned with control of pupils, classroom atmosphere, avoidance of confrontation with pupils), and *idealist* (where mixed ability offered egalitarian opportunities, where comprehensive schools could become truly comprehensive). Although these are perspectives on a particular practical issue (mixed ability), it can be seen that the beliefs and attitudes held have deeper roots. What Ball's study does is to show the particular contours a structure of feeling take when they are drawn upon in the consideration of particular problems. The *academic* perspective clearly emerges from the achievement/individualism structure of feeling, the *idealist* from social welfare/egalitarianism, and the *disciplinary* from a pragmatic accommodation of both.

A wider ranging survey which illuminates the concept of structure of feeling is Michael Rutter's research.[23] He studied twelve inner London comprehensive schools involving 2000 pupils throughout their secondary schooling. His findings marked differences between the schools in terms of pupils' academic achievement, behaviour in school and delinquency. It seems clear that some schools affected their pupils more positively than others (better exam results and behaviour, lower delinquency rates). Rutter examined a large number of features of school life and his work would seem to suggest that 'ethos' or 'climate' – what in our terms would include structures of feeling – significantly affect such outcomes. He reports such climates as 'school processes' and found that better results (academic and behavioural) were obtained in schools with an 'academic emphasis' (careful planning and organisation of work), with cooperative and productive classroom atmospheres, with sanctioning systems that favoured rewards rather than punishments, and with an emphasis on pupil participation and responsibilities. Clearly, such emphases, with their attendant practices (such as 'lessons not ending early', 'public commendation for work and behaviour', 'assembly participation', and so on) suggest underpinning and pervading structures of feeling which influence pupil attitude, achievement and behaviour.

Rutter reports 'a very strong and highly consistent correlation (0.92) between overall school process and pupil behaviour'.[24] Whilst we may question his selection and measurement of these processes, there is little doubt that he is providing some scientific validation of those intuitions of most teachers that the differences between schools or between classrooms can be sensed in the climate of feeling that exists in each; and that ethos plays a very significant part in determining behaviour and attainment. Rutter's measures have many of the defects of positivistic research; approaches to school ethos through structures of feeling require more than scientific method to do justice to the cultural complexity of schools. Nevertheless the importance of *Fifteen Thousand Hours* cannot be understated as countering sociological pessimism about the influence of schools on pupils; school *can* make a difference, and its ethos contributes to success or failure:

> Schools can do much to foster good behaviour and attainments, and
> . . . even in a disadvantaged area, schools can be a force for the good.[25]

Christopher Ormell's analytical, rather than empirical, contribution can also be seen as concerned with structures of feeling.[26] He identifies two overriding imperatives in education: conservation and stability, innovation and change. His preoccupation is with values and he suggests that those traditionally supported included religion, character-building, personal advancement, learning, traditional culture, manners, socialisation. In contrast, those which have risen in prominence recently include non-traditional culture, doing your own thing, creativity, independence of judgement, thinking, expression. His own list of educational values include encouragement of wholeness, balance, life, coherence, comprehensiveness, general varieties of understanding, awareness, constructivity, creativity, expression, thought and problem-solving capacity. Ormell's list can be reconceptualised as structures of feeling: systems of belief, of preferences, which constitute the springs of action for the individual. Although his thesis lacks the tight empirical grounding of Ball or Willis, it nonetheless is highly suggestive of how the concept of structure of feeling can make a contribution to both theory and practical investigations.

In Ronald King's original and regrettably under-remarked research into infant classrooms can be seen further evidence of the existence and power of structures of feeling.[27] Over a period of three years King spent about 600 hours in direct observation of classrooms in three infant schools. The patterns and regularities he recorded showed that infant schooling is a clearly recognisable social world. This fact would be banal (after all, any perceptive observer recognises that after five minutes in an infant class) if it were not for King's attribution of those regularities to what he calls the ideology of infant teachers. The ideology has all the characteristics of what I call structure of feeling, for it constitutes a set of beliefs or assumptions about young children and their learning which informed, guided and explained individual teachers' actions. These taken for granted beliefs ensured the patterns and regularities King observed, for they resulted in agreed ways of doing things. The structure of feeling was drawn on as a resource by infant teachers and King's endeavour can be seen as identifying that structure and locating its more formal expression in written sources: letters to parents, notes for staff guidance, books used in infant schools, and the Plowden Report *Children and their Primary Schools*.[28] King distinguishes four elements that comprise this essentially child-centred structure of feeling: developmentalism, individualism, play as learning and childhood innocence. *Developmentalism* is the Plowden natural growth model: children pass through a naturally ordered sequence of physical, emotional, intellectual and social growth. Thus, teachers' actions were much informed by a notion of readiness ('You're too young to do those sums'; 'Take that back, dear, and tell your teacher you are not ready to change yet'). *Individualism* stresses the uniqueness of each child and King records in detail how well the teachers 'knew' their children and strove to take account of what they saw as particular characteristics of each individual. *Play as learning*, officially endorsed by the Plowden Report, has a long history, not simply in its advocates in the infant school movement (Pestalozzi, Froebel, Montessori, the McMillan sisters and Susan Isaacs) but in all child-centred theories of learning. Its related beliefs are *interest* ('follow the child's interests'), *happiness* ('Let me see a smile. A good big one!') and *busy-ness* ('Let being busy be your golden rule!'). But for King, the fourth element, *childhood innocence* is the central component of infant teachers' ideology: the notion that young children cannot be blamed for their actions

('I'm sure he didn't mean to do it'). It is this belief that marks them off from other teachers and which makes an infant classroom unlike other classrooms.

King argues that this ideology shapes teachers' actions. For him, 'the reality of the classroom for the teacher was constructed through her ideology.'

Thus King's work can be seen as asserting that structures of feeling not only influence how teachers see the world (their pupils and classroom) but, further, that these beliefs and perceptions become *self-confirming*. Using W. I. Thomas' notion of 'definition of the situation' (that is, 'if men define situations as real, they are real in their consequences'), King shows that what the teachers believe, they strive to make come true, and, by their actions, they create that 'truth'. The structure of feeling becomes reality itself. This is a very strong claim, but the importance of King's contribution cannot be over-estimated. For all its weaknesses (particularly its concept of ideology, its relativism, its confusions over 'innocence', and so on),[29] it is one of the few researches which systematically and convincingly examines the relationships between observed classroom practices and 'absent' structures. It conveys vividly the 'feeling tone' of infant classrooms and shows clearly how taken-for-granted, often unexamined beliefs have powerfully practical consequences as they are drawn upon, expressed and reconfirmed in infant teachers' actions.

Above I have set out three dominant structures of feeling present in schooling and I have shown how certain empirical studies illuminate aspects of those structures. Clearly other structures of feeling exist which do not fit so easily into these three categories. Racism and sexism are two prime examples.[30] There is not space here to trace their contours; rather, in conclusion I shall identify a structure of feeling, *instrumental rationality*, that has received comparatively little attention in the literature on schooling although its impact on education is increasingly powerful.

Instrumental rationality signifies a preoccupation with 'How to do it?' questions rather than with questions of 'Why do it?' or 'Where are we going?' It is thus concerned with means rather than ends, with efficiency more than consideration of purposes. In schools one manifestation is a stress on management and organization at the expense of consideration of 'What is education for?'

The identification of, and challenge to, instrumental reason has long been associated with the Frankfurt School (see note 3, Chapter 4, page 59). The work of the School, together with the current writings of Jurgen Habermas, represents a conscious attempt to rethink Marxism as critical theory.[31]

Both economic determinism and positivism are severely questioned as the focus of critical theory shifts to an examination of ideology, of language and of the distortions of thought and social practice. Critical theory claims that it enables both enlightenment and emancipation. By establishing reason as its central category the links between theory and practice are reaffirmed: seeing things clearly can effect transformation to more just social relationships. The Frankfurt School saw *instrumental rationality* as a disposition of thought and feeling underpinning positivism, fascism and capitalism and as such leading to the eclipse of reason. Two concepts of reason were distinguished: *instrumental (or technical or subjective)* which referred to the adequacy of specific means to attain predetermined ends; and *substantive (or objective)* reason which concerned itself with the worthiness of ends themselves. Habermas, for example, distinguishes between the Greek notions of *theoria* and *techne*. The former is a concern with the just and the good life, with the full integration of theory and practice; the latter is a technical approach to politics and life, concerned with the means not the ends of living, with the *prediction and control* of human affairs at the expense of consideration of the value of ends. For the Frankfurt School the modern world is characterised, in belief, thought and practice, by instrumental reason. The quite astonishing growth of science and technology is evidence of how far technical capacity has outrun the consideration of purposes. The triumph of technical reason is evidenced daily in many ways, from nuclear weapons to television advertising. In schooling it may be thought that instrumental reason has been challenged and overcome by the progressive movement, the concern for aims and objectives, the increased attention to pupils' social and emotional growth. But in the harsh climate of the 1980s it can be seen that such developments are themselves massively countered as instrumental reason emerges in different, sharper forms. Marcuse's *One Dimensional Man* in whom technical rationality is dominant has re-emerged in all spheres of life, and with biting impact in education, with calls for efficiency, measurement and the 'value for money' movement of the New Conservatism.

This structure of feeling is compounded by the tremendous decline in morale among teachers faced with sharply reduced resources, fierce critics and increasing demands for accountability. Teachers see themselves increasingly beleaguered, increasingly under pressure from inside and outside school to produce results. Those 'results' signify efficiency measured in economic terms rather than by educational principles. Indices are the unrelenting growth of examinations, the abandonment of the Robbins' principle, the creation of the Assessment of Performance Unit, and (after enduring two decades of the Left's criticism of the liberal ideology) the increasing cynicism of the Right towards education's worthwhileness. As Professor Wragg commented in 1982:

> The Prime Minister visited the DES towards the end of the year and was so unspeakably awful to everyone present, and so unable to listen to what anyone tried to say when she demanded to know what education had achieved with all the money spent on it, that friend and foe alike were left shaking their heads with disbelief.[32]

The structure of feeling that underpinned Payment by Results has come full circle. Its impact can be shown through a single example from an English county. A Bedfordshire report reveals that in 1982 half the county's headteachers expected pupils' achievements to fall because of low morale among teachers. The effect of spending cuts on teacher confidence was dramatic; as the Chief Education Officer reported

> When teachers look at their job security, school security, resources and increasing social stresses within the job, then confidence is an early victim. To retain some morale is becoming increasingly difficult.[33]

Such a remark is highly significant both in its own right and for the structural perspective of this book. For it not only pinpoints with deadly accuracy the state of affairs which exists in schools but it also shows clearly how individuals experience and express the sombre pressures of the social and feeling structures in which they are embedded. Such climates or structures of feeling are not subject to precise measurement, but they are readily evidenced at all levels from direct personal experience, through institutional ethos, to the pervasive beliefs and values of a whole culture or society. We sense it in ourselves; we recognise it in a classroom or school; and we acknowledge it in a community or culture. Structures of feeling are rarely homogeneous or simple, they are always shifting in particular forms of expression, but there is no doubting their existence or power.

NOTES

1 White and Brockington (1983).
2 Raymond Williams has long been preoccupied with the concept of structures of feeling. A recent collection of his essays indicates his development of the notion: see Williams (1980).
3 Williams (1973, pp. 8–10).
4 Williams (1977, p. 132).
5 By 'emergent' structures of feeling, Williams means new ways of seeing and experiencing. He analyses Ibsen's revolutionary impact on European drama as an example of an emergent structure. An approach which (without using the terminology) analyses emergent, dominant and residual structures of feeling in English culture from 1850–1980 is Weiner (1981). He argues forcibly that middle-class ambivalence towards industrialisation has led to our economic decline. His book is an essay on the feeling structures of English culture and, although it contains only a few pages on education, merits close consideration by teachers.
6 Schutz (1967).
7 Giddens (1982).
8 Weber (1904), and see also Tawney (1926).
9 Schutz (1967). Alfred Schutz' work has been mediated by Peter Berger and Thomas Luckmann (1967) (a work owing much to Husserl's concept of the 'natural attitude').
10 Giddens (1979, p. 57).
11 White and Brockington (1983, p. 41).
12 Hargreaves (1967).
13 Hargreaves (1982).
14 Hargreaves (1982, p. 52).
15 Willis (1977).
16 Hargreaves (1982, p. 87).
17 Hargreaves (1982, p. 100).
18 Gibson (1981b).
19 Grace (1978, p. 10).
20 Willis (1977).
21 Ball (1981).
22 Becker (1961, pp. 33–4).
23 Rutter et al. (1979).
24 Rutter et al. (1979, p. 142).
25 Rutter et al. (1979, p. 205).
26 Ormell (1980, pp. 71–95).
27 King (1978).
28 Department of Education and Science (1967).
29 Gibson (1979).
30 The extensive literature on sexism and racism in education is

evidence of the complex structures of feeling represented. See the papers in Centre for Contemporary Cultural Studies (1982); Barton and Walker (1983); Walker and Barton (1983); Stanworth (1983).
31 Three books which are good introductions to the ideas of the Frankfurt School are Held (1982); Jay (1973); Geuss (1981).
32 *The Times Educational Supplement*, 31 December 1982 (p. 32).
33 *The Guardian*, 31 December 1982 (p. 2).

6 Structuralism and Literature

For many teachers in schools, the arguments at Cambridge over structuralism seem remote, irrelevant. What, after all, have debates about little known French theorists and theories to do with everyday school life? Even teachers of English found 'the McCabe affair' far distant from their practical concerns of marking books and preparing students for external examinations. One such teacher commented that the whole business seemed to take place in another world, watched by outsiders

> . . . with the same kind of fascination and curiosity which the Royal Family provoke. Important matters were clearly at stake, but for the average English teacher those matters were remote from his or her day-to-day practice.[1]

If structuralism is impenetrable and obscure for teachers, it seems doubly so for pupils and their parents. For many, the requirements of school English are already far removed from their experience and interests. Coronation Street or Conan the Barbarian, James Bond or *The Sun* newspaper rarely figure in the school curriculum. If they do, the approach is frequently hostile, designed to show the triviality or worthlessness of such widely viewed, widely read manifestations of popular culture. Against such a background, heated discussions at an ancient university about literary theory hold neither meaning nor significance. If Shakespeare has only a tenuous hold in Scunthorpe, structuralism has no chance at all.

But what is clear is that the Cambridge English faculty dispute was not a storm in an academic teacup, an insular, local row between irritable dons. As preceding chapters have shown, structuralism reaches into all areas of human life from the most mundane to the most self-conscious. The Cambridge affair, ostensibly concerning methods of teaching literature, goes far deeper. Literature is central to education; reading is crucial to schooling: but structuralism raises fundamental issues. It is about the shaping of consciousness itself: how we come to see the world, in all its aspects, as we do. For most teachers and their pupils there is a 'matter-of-factness', a 'givenness' about all they do, about the world they inhabit. The importance of structuralism is in questioning that givenness, probing as it does the common-sense assumptions which prevail about the naturalness of our activities and perceptions. In this chapter, I will examine the specific case of structuralism and literature not only because argument is fiercest in this area (see note 1, Chapter 1, page 12), but because of literature's centrality in schooling and because structuralist method here offers fruitful analogies for understanding social life itself.

The relations of structuralism and literature need to be understood in the context of different approaches to the study of literature. It is possible to distinguish four major approaches, all practised at university level, but very differently represented in the teaching of literature in schools. The first (with a long history pre-dating the institutionalisation of English studies in universities) is that of scholarship on texts: patient, scrupulous research which attempts to establish what the author originally wrote. Shakespeare is the classic example and a glance at any editor's introduction to a Shakespeare play reveals the scale, difficulties and interdisciplinarity of the enterprise. One well-known example illustrates the problems involved: does Hamlet speak of 'solid', 'sullied', or 'sallied' flesh? This concern to establish the text is an activity for career scholars and researchers. It is not the business of undergraduate students in higher education, and in schools it is no part of the pupils' activities: for them, the text is given.

The second approach, a product of the 1920s, its origin attributed to I. A. Richards, and much associated with F. R. Leavis, is a method of study that has been influential at all levels of education. It can be called the human encounter with literature, the response to the text. Pioneered by Richards' exercises in practical criticism, it concerns itself with how the individual responds when faced with (most typically) a poem, or novel, or play. Here, in closely focused examination of the text, emotion and intelligence uniquely combine to produce a judgment, an evaluation. Key words in such an approach are 'authenticity', 'sincerity', 'critical awareness'. Its assumption is that there is a correlation between the individual's feelings and the quality of the work. Both responses and texts can therefore be ranked in terms of their depth, sincerity, humanity. The 'educated reader's' response is somehow truer, more perceptive, more authentic; the capability for discrimination is increased and the capacity for responding to great works expanded. 'Great works' are, indeed, the central, undisputed focus of such an approach, and the approach itself can identify them. 'Literature' and 'great works' become interchangeable terms as the moral worthiness of text (and responses) are scrupulously, minutely revealed. George Eliot, Henry James are exemplary, and 'revaluation' (significantly, the title of one of F. R. Leavis' books) admits others (notably D. H. Lawrence, T. S. Eliot) to the canon, to the 'great tradition' of English Literature. The encounter between reader and text is a moral one, and one which transcends local, temporal circumstance. In its 'purest' form (for example, in Richards' book *Practical Criticism*) history, context, author all disappear as the student is presented with only a text (with no mention of author, date or other information) and required to respond to that alone. The encounter is uniquely between the poem and the sensibility of the reader: the finer the sensibility the more refined and discriminating the judgment, the truer the assessment. The capital 'L' of 'Literature' marks its membership off from other coarser, mundane or trivial writings.

The language of this second approach is everyday, conversational, nontechnical; theory is eschewed. More than that, theory is rejected, despised. It is unnecessary and comes between the reader and the text, sullying the response, impeding common sense. 'This is so, isn't it?' was Leavis' practical, down to earth, anti-theory method. However, as the approach developed it proved impossible to keep comparison (other poems, possible authors, historical background) out of such responses. Greater acknowledgment was therefore made of the contexts in which any poem or play is embedded. Nonetheless, attention remained squarely upon the text itself: literature was 'foregrounded', history and society 'backgrounded'. Knowledge of society was valuable for the illumination it afforded of the text. Our understanding of Elizabethan England enriched our response to Shakespeare, but the text itself was nonetheless transcendent, accessible to the discriminating intellect and emotion. In this approach the proper study of literature is literature itself, for it is not a means to an end, not a vehicle to understand society, but an end in itself. Much was made of the educational implications of the approach, for it saw reading literature and moral development as intertwined, mutually dependent. The moral qualities present in the work of art (novel, play, poem) revealed by 'true' reading, an appropriate response, became synonymous with education: they *were* the ends of education. At the levels of both higher education and schooling this approach has been the most powerful influence on English studies.[2]

The third approach alters the balance between literature and history, literature and society. If traditional scholarship and the human response approach used historical and social evidence in the service of the text, now the terms of the relationship shift. Literature is studied in order to identify its role and function in society; to discover the correspondences between *its* forms and other societal forms; to find what it can tell us *about* society. The language of this approach draws heavily on the social sciences; in marked contrast to the human response approach it favours theory (often Marxist). In its strongest version, literary study is used as a tool for social analysis; literature loses its privileged status as its 'mystery' and 'art' are stripped away. It becomes a means not simply for understanding but for improving and serving society. Some Marxist approaches (but certainly not all and certainly not Karl Marx himself) take this latter stance, where no longer is 'art for art's sake' acceptable, but rather 'art for society's sake'. Dickens, for example, can be pressed into service primarily as a tool to criticise Victorian capitalism (an activity which the 'human response' school finds insensitive).

However, the relationship between literature and society has long been a major feature of the English critical tradition. Leavis' writing, for example, is typified by moral and social criticism based on a particular view of 'organic' society. Imbued with notions of social health, right relationships, for Leavis literature was indeed social criticism. Jane Austen and George Eliot exposed the hypocrisies of current social practices. But for Leavis, as for the still dominant tradition of literary study, literature is securely foregrounded. In contrast, radical expressions of the changed balance of literature and society can be seen in the work of Terry Eagleton (1978) and Arnold Kettle (1967), and in recent work at the University of Birmingham's Centre for Contemporary Cultural Studies (Hall, 1980). However, the writer who has done most to shift the balance whilst still respecting the integrity and independence of literature is Raymond Williams. His explorations of the relationships between literature and society have been at once delicate, sophisticated, radical and seminal. No other writer has been so influential in opening up fresh fields of enquiry in the relationships between literature and society. His abiding pre-occupation with cultural forms and their connection with the material and ideological forms of society represents a distinctively British reworking of the nature of literary studies.[3] In schools there is a well-established tradition (due largely to the influence of F. R. Leavis) of social criticism and of the opposition of literary and certain social values ('getting and spending we lay waste our powers'). Hostility to consumerism, to the mass media, even to science, is characteristic. Nonetheless, more radically critical approaches, Marxist analyses or the study of correspondences in social and literary forms are rarely if at all present. Such approaches are deferred until the stage of higher education where they frequently encounter strong opposition.

The fourth approach to English studies is one concerned with the internal systems and mechanisms of literature; its questions are: 'How does this text work?' 'What sort of text is it?' It analyses the world of literature, identifying conventions, genres, concepts, methods that are distinctively literary. This approach springs from a very long tradition. The study of rhetoric, which loomed so large in the classical and Renaissance worlds and which was for long one of the main strands of the school curriculum, is its ancestor. In one form it survived and flourishes in schools. Generations of examination candidates faced with practical critic- ism have striven to show how rhythm, rhyme, repetition, imag- ery, association, verse form and so on all contribute to the poem's effect (or how plot, character, point of view and so on contribute to the novel). In this form it is held to be complementary but subservient to the human response approach. The literary devices identified contribute to the richness of the work, but its moral seriousness, its imaginative power, or our enjoyment of it, trans- cend such mechanics. Indeed, most textbooks which set out such techniques do so a touch apologetically, nodding as they do to Wordsworth's 'we murder to dissect', acknowledging the super- iority of intuitive, 'true' response. Thus, as most school pupils experience it, this approach is the handmaid of the celebratory, deferential stance to great works favoured by the human response school. It has very little to do with theory and in its conventional form it poses no threat to 'literature', accepting it uncritically as a given and narrow canon of works by English authors.[4]

But the alternative form of the fourth approach *is* threatening, radical, subversive even. It is literary structuralism, which, far from celebrating literature, far from making evaluations as to moral worth, questions traditional notions of what *counts* as literature, concerns itself centrally not with response and intui- tion, not with evaluation, but with the *system* that makes literature possible. Such activities, and the very self-conscious theorising which characterises structuralism, are regarded with great suspicion by the majority of English teachers who have been socialised into what might be called the Leavisian tradition (or, more simply, to a tradition that stresses a common-sense, respectful, closely textually focused, untheoretical approach to a given set of 'great works').

Literary Structuralism

There are many varieties of literary structuralism; indeed it is fashionable (but inappropriate) to speak of 'post-structuralism' as if structuralism itself belonged to a past era. As we noted in Chapter I, it is an intellectual movement which flourishes in mainland Europe, particularly France, where attitudes to theory are far more positive than in England. Its most influential introduction to Britain and the United States was through Jonathan Culler's *Structuralist Poetics* published in 1975. Until the much-publicised McCabe affair at Cambridge in 1980–1 brought it to the attention of a wider audience, literary structuralism was the active concern of relatively few critics and scholars in higher education. Among these, the best known are probably Frank Kermode, David Lodge and Geoffrey Strickland, all of whom bring particularly English sensibilities to their study of structuralism, demonstrating its limitations and potentialities.[5] The glare of publicity occasioned by the McCabe case came as a surprise and, as Kermode (until 1982 a Professor of English at Cambridge University) remarked at the time, 'literary theory is somewhat bewilderingly in the news'. Readers who desire an entertaining insight into what a mild (that is, English) version of literary structuralism looks like should read David Lodge's essay 'Oedipuss: or the practice and theory of narrative'.[6] Here, Lodge examines one of his own short stories and discovers its structure to be that of the story of Oedipus. A family, going on holiday, must leave its cat behind to be fed by neighbours. The husband, rushing back from buying the catfood, accidentally runs over and kills the cat. Lodge is struck by the similarity of his story to the legend of Oedipus who has left Corinth to avoid killing his father and marrying his mother but, through that action, inevitably commits both crimes. Lodge's husband-father kills the cat in his action (buying food) intended to keep it alive. Lodge is impressed by this correspondence (discovered *after* writing his story) and by other structuralist elements, concluding:

> . . . it is not so much man that speaks language as language that speaks man; not so much the writer who writes narrative as narrative that writes the writer.

Such structuralist claims ('language speaks man'; 'narrative writes the writer') are anathema to followers of Leavis. Structuralism's decentring of the subject is seen here at full force. The centrality of the individual, of genius, of creativity, on which the 'human response' school insists, is frontally challenged. Translated to the realm of schooling it becomes 'society determines the pupil', 'schooling makes the teachers'. However, Lodge's work is of interest because he actually engages in structural analysis of literature, demonstrating, by considering particular works, how the method provides insights. This is in contrast to much structuralist writing which concerns itself more with theorising about structuralism than with actually practising it. Lodge shows that structuralism is primarily a method, not concerned with the meaning, value or interpretation of a work but with the devices that enable it to be written, that is to say with its structural characteristics. What marks him off from more committed (dogmatic?) European structuralists is that his writing is not only accessible, avoiding excess of technical terms, but that in his criticism he finds it impossible to avoid questions of meaning, interpretation and value. A comparison of his writing with that of Roman Jakobson or Jacques Derrida[7] reveals the very wide range of structuralist approaches to literature. For all its variety, literary structuralism is most easily understood by considering the characteristics of structuralism identified in Chapter i, which are present, with changed emphasis, in every type. In what follows I shall identify respectively how literary structuralism employs the notions of wholeness, self-regulation, transformation, relationships, synchronic analysis and decentring of the subject. This last element leads to a discussion of post-structuralism or deconstruction.

Wholeness

Structuralism views literature as a system or structure, a totality with its own conventions and traditions, explicable in terms of itself. This whole takes precedence over individual authors or readers or texts. When Lodge remarks 'narrative . . . writes the writer', or when Gabriel Josipovici asserts 'the genre quite as much as John Milton . . . is responsible for Lycidas'[8] they are drawing attention to the whole, the totality, which governs individual (i.e. the author's) action. The task of the literary structuralist is to identify, within this closed world, the conventions, devices, methods that make it work, which enable authors to write, readers to read. The structured elements of the whole may be such familiar ones as plot, character, symbol, or less familiarly, codes or binary oppositions, or the principles of metaphor and metonymy. Such structures underpin a whole range of structuralist activities: classifying within and between literary genres; identifying the fundamental dramatic situations; revealing the structures of fairy tales and myths; mapping the laws and functions of folk tales, demonstrating the various ways in which signs or language create an illusion of reality and hence convey meaning (the structuralist concept of *vraisemblance*). The analogy here is with Saussure's *langue*: the whole that makes speech possible.

Self-regulation

It is the Saussurian notion of the *arbitrary character of the sign* which allows the structuralist to search not for meaning, but for method. His pursuit of the rules governing literary expression can be undertaken within the whole that is literature, without reference to an outside world. As Jonathan Culler puts it:

> Rather than a criticism which discovers or assigns meanings it would be a poetics which strives to define the conditions of meaning . . .[9]

Clearly the 'conditions' are to be found in other texts, in the genres and conventions of literature itself:

> . . . the analyst's task is not simply to describe a corpus but to account for the structure and meaning that items of the corpus have for those who have assimilated the rules and norms of the system . . . the basic task is to render as explicit as possible the conventions responsible for the production of attested effects.[10]

Here is clearly the notion of *self-regulation*, for the conventions of literature are 'responsible' for its effect. Structuralism concerns itself with the 'literariness' of literature: significance lies in the literary laws, patterns and devices that make the individual text and the whole system work. Such concern issues in the formal analyses of Roman Jakobson. Here he is on Shakespeare's Sonnet 129, 'Th' expense of Spirit':

> The four strophic units exhibit three kinds of binary correspondences: (1) alternation (abab), which ties together the two *odd* strophes (I, III) and opposes them to the even strophes which are tied in turn to each other (II, IV); (2) framing (abba) which brings together the enclosing *outer* strophes (I, IV) and opposes them to the two enclosed, mutually related *inner* strophes (II, III); (3) neighbourhood (aabb), which builds pairs of anterior (I, II) and posterior (III, IV) strophes opposed to each other.[11]

And his chapter headings arranged as binary oppositions reveal his structuralist preoccupation with theory construction as they claim to identify the underlying structures: 'Odd against even', 'Outer against inner', 'Anterior against posterior', 'Couplets against quatrains'. Any text is subordinate to the structure; it is the outcome of that structure; the enterprise is one of revealing the codes which govern literary discourse. Particular self-regulating structures can also be found which govern an individual author's work. Tzvetan Todorov, for instance, searches for 'the figure in Henry James's Carpet, the primary plan on which everything else depends, as it appears in each one of his works'. He finds this 'invariant factor' by considering all James' tales and he confidently reveals the structural formula: 'James's tales are based on the quest for an absolute and absent cause.'[12]

Transformation

It is in terms of such 'primal plans' for individual authors, and in terms of its internal laws and mechanisms for literature itself, that structuralists explain how *transformations* take place. An individual author is governed by both particular and general structures as his own work develops. Those structures guarantee change. Within the whole that is literature, both practices and conventions are changed, for there is an internal dynamic such that, as literature comments upon itself, so it modifies itself. The dialectic between any work and other works is such that transformation is effected by the system. Literature has a life of its own with its own inbuilt mechanisms for development. For structuralists it is an active sign system achieving its own transformations: Shakespeare is to be explained through existing conventions which are transformed as he draws on them; modernism arises from the nineteenth century novel. All are subject to the deep structures which govern literary practice and which ensure both continuity and change. The notion of transformation is not confined to the writing of texts, it is central to the act of reading itself. Structuralism maintains that each reader reconstructs the text anew. Rutherford's comment on reading is rich in Piagetian resonances:

> Reading . . . is a confrontation between the possibilities of the text and the expectations and needs of readers . . . it is activity, construction, play, rather than passivity, reception, contemplation.[13]

But for a structuralist those activities take place within, and are the outcome of, structural laws. Transformations take place at both the level of the system and the individual with both being subject to those laws.

Relationships

Throughout all structuralist writing can be seen the emphasis on the *relationships* that exist within the totality that is literature. Structuralist analysis of literature, as of other practices, concerns itself little with individuals or things, but with the relationships of word to language, of text to genre, convention, device: to the whole that is literature. *Lear* and *Look Back in Anger* alike are to be explained by their structural origins. As Todorov puts it: 'Structuralism is a scientific method implying an interest in impersonal laws and forms, of which existing objects are only the realisation.' Following the principle that elements have significance *only* through their relationships, literary structuralism seeks the relationships of a particular text to the forms that make up literature.

To use the ideas of Derrida, it seeks those absences which give meaning to presences. In these 'absent' networks reside the deep structures of literature that enable writers to write and readers to read. Once again, in this stress on relationships we can see the neglect, even dismissal, of meaning and interpretation. It is not difficult to see why English critics and scholars raised in the tradition of F. R. Leavis react so strongly against the priorities directly stated in Culler's task for structuralists:

> . . . to reconstruct the conventions which enable physical objects or events to have meaning . . . to formulate the pertinent distinctions and relations among elements as well as the rules governing their possibility of combination . . . not (to) discover what a sequence means or

produce a new interpretation of it but tries to determine the nature of the system underlying the event.[15]

Synchronic analysis

This 'system' is to be studied as a *snapshot* (or *synchronically*). The present, rather than the past is what matters, and a study of how the words on the page relate to each other and how the text is realised through literary devices effectively banishes history. For all its emphasis on transformation, structuralism emphasises that literature, like the Saussurian *langue*, should be conceptualised as wholes that exist at (and as) particular 'moments'. These moments include an entire network of relationships. The operations which enable texts to be written and read become 'present' through synchronic analysis in which the past is incorporated into the present, made manifest in the network that is literature. Such, at least, is the theory. In practice, few structuralists achieve such ideal analyses – and certainly no British practitioner does.

Decentring the subject

The most radical form of structuralism banishes not only history but also the author and the reader (in spite of all the emphasis put on the latter's recreation of the text at each reading). Julia Kristeva asserts:

> It is no longer 'I' who reads; the impersonal time of regularity, of the grid, of harmony, takes up this 'I' which is in fragments from having read; *one* reads.[16]

The Anglo-Saxon mind finds it difficult to comprehend such a remark; it is far from our experience and our taken-for-granted assumptions. It, and Culler's comment on it, are deeply threatening to our notions of common sense, to our feelings of personal identity:

> The subject who reads is constituted by a series of conventions, the grids of regularity and intersubjectivity. The empirical 'I' is dispersed among these conventions which take over from him in the act of reading.[17]

What we see here is that literary structuralism, like all structuralism, rigidly, necessarily, *decentres the subject*. The price that must be paid in according the priority of the system is the subordination (or even disappearance) of the individual. Author and reader become mere agents of the structures of literature, passive tools of literary codes. As Catherine Belsey notes:

> Roland Barthes has specifically proclaimed the death of the author; and Jacques Lacan, Louis Althusser and Jacques Derrida have all from various positions questioned the humanist assumption that subjectivity, the individual mind or inner being, is the source of meaning and action.[18]

Signs, rather than men, are dominant, as neither the intentions nor the setting of the author are of interest or relevance. For it follows that if a work belongs to a system, the writer, however much a genius, is forced to follow the codes and conventions of that system. His work exists only by permission and creation of the totality of literature itself.

Post-structuralism

In the decentring just noted we glimpse the structuralism of the 'deconstructionists',[19] the post-structuralism which clearly goes against the common-sense assumptions of the great majority of readers. I, and almost every reader of this book assume that an author intends to tell a story or express himself; that he does so in a poem, play, or novel, and so tells the truth in some way about human nature or about the world so that the reader can grasp and share the author's insights, perceptions. Such common-sense simplicities are not acceptable to the post-structuralists who carry their theorising well beyond any earlier limits. (It is interesting to note that even such a structuralist advocate as Professor David Lodge declares himself baffled by much of the current structuralist texts – small hope for the common reader!) This most radical element of structuralist thought does not simply lack interest in the *meaning* of a text as opposed to its internal devices, but denies that any objective meaning is possible. Like all structuralism, post-structuralism is a heterogeneous movement, but we can discern four elements: a stress on closed systems, on plurality of meaning, on the impossibility of truth claims, and on the impossibility of meaning itself.

The self-enclosed nature of systems is by now a familiar idea to us. It can be seen in Barthes' description of fashion and literature as:

> . . . systems whose function is not to communicate an objective, external meaning which exists prior to the system, but only to create a functioning equilibrium, a movement of signification . . . they signify 'nothing'; their essence is in the process of signification, not in what they signify.[20]

Here, literature will be replaced by semiotics, for writing – any writing, Shakespeare or advertising jingles – is merely different parts of a system of signs which can be studied to discover how they work.

Plurality of meaning might seem a familiar and acceptable idea to English readers who have grown up with the notion that great literature offers a richness, a plenitude of interpretation. We never finish with Shakespeare. But the post-structuralists go well beyond this, for, linking it with the notion of the impossibility of truth claims, all chance of judging the quality of a work disappears:

> Texts can be read in many ways; each text contains within itself the possibility of an infinite set of structures, and to privilege some by setting up a system of rules to generate them is a blatantly prescriptive and ideological move.[21]

Here the door is open to dispense with any notion of a canon of literature, a set of great works, for such a view treats all claims to truth as delusions. Under such a view literature would lose its implicit capital 'L' and teachers could no longer find reasons to defend the study of Shakespeare as against Ian Fleming, or *The Beano*. The human response approach to literature is fundamentally undermined as relativism rules.

Deconstruction's final move to the very impossibility of meaning itself is made as it 'refuses to identify the force of literature with any concept of embodied meaning', and is seen in the work of Derrida whose 'theory of language . . . teaches the dearth of meaning'.[22] Such a view bewilders conventional scholars and readers. It certainly bewilders me but it can be quickly dealt with, for if no meaning can be established and truth has no relevance, there is no reason why any attention should be paid to these deconstructionists themselves. By their own admission, any reading is possible, none more valid than another. So why bother to read them at all? Such a dismissal is perhaps too easy and in making it I am only too aware of the truth of much structuralist theory, for I recognise in it the grip on my own mind of particular ways of thinking: the Anglo-Saxon empirical tradition and the influence of Dr Leavis.

If structuralism is characterised by its preference for grand theory, post-structuralism must be noted for its sweeping assertions, its excitement and inconsistencies. Its association with events in Paris of the late 1960s is significant: stimulation and challenge, a wilful desire to shake and shock, and a fundamental questioning of the most taken for granted assumptions. Like Marxist criticism, its stance is one of irreverence: works of art are not held in awe, but are to be demystified, exposed, explained. As we have seen, it denies the distinction between literature and other forms of writing, arguing that the codes it postulates apply to all language use, to all sign systems. It is this lack of respect for the mystery of creativity that Denis Donoghue inveighed against in his 1982 Reith Lectures. In its preference for modernism, for resistant, fragmented, uncooperative, uninterpretable, 'unreadable' texts, deconstruction echoes its own values, and reveals its cultural diagnosis. It embraces the 'principle of resistance' employed by modern writers:

For literature is essentially the discourse of doubt rather than of affirmation.[23]

Where structuralism sought literary codes which gave pattern and significance, deconstruction abandons any possibility of coherence in its sheer relativism and its stress on 'the abysm of words' which denies stable, objective or true interpretation as either relevant or possible in literary studies. The self-indulgent excesses of post-structuralism need not delay us, standing as they do as speculative theorising that relishes its self-contradiction. In its determined exclusion through its private language of all but its own small clique of priests and faithful, it seems to be, in Harold Bloom's phrase, no more than a 'serene linguistic nihilism'.

But the whole complex enterprise that is literary structuralism cannot be dismissed or disregarded. It contains powerful insights as well as self-evident flaws. Its demand for the priority of analytic over intuitive approaches to literature requires attention, even if the practical outcome is likely to be some attempt to accommodate the two. The claims made for it are far too large; all too often its analyses of particular texts are remarkably unconvincing although with Kermode and Lodge there are notable successes. Its Achilles' heel is in its too-close adherence to its insistence on the merely arbitrary connection between signified and signifier which results, for many structuralists, in a neglect of reference to any world external to literature. Such a view quite simply is untenable and any structural analysis which insists rigidly upon such a principle lapses into indefensible solipsism. As Benveniste has shown, the relationships between language and the world are never simply contingent.[24] Structuralism's concentration on pattern and symmetry at the expense of truth and meaning is reductive, diminishing, trivialising. There is a constant curious contrast between structuralism's idea of the intrinsic intelligibility of human affairs and the sense of dehumanisation that is so evident in many of its literary investigations. Its predilection for structure and its critical attitude to humanism square awkwardly with any expanded, integrative notion of 'wholeness'.

Literary structuralism's search for systems and structures that have priority, dominance, control over the individual is a gross denial of the self-evident competence of both author and reader. Like all structuralism it lacks a theory of the competent human actor. Any development of structural analysis must accommodate itself to the fact of human capability and knowledgeability. Further, like all structuralism, its rejection of history is a merely theoretical move that can only weaken its contribution to literary studies. Finally, its claim to scientific status is, like the similar claims of all grand theories about human behaviour, mere hubris, an empty assertion that is in reality only a misguided attempt to raise its own status. It is not surprising therefore that structuralism, in almost all forms, has met with opposition and ridicule from the scholars who work in the mainstream tradition of literature. George Watson's account of (and dismissal of) structuralism meets with widespread approval.[25] But whilst there is opposition too from Marxists (to whom the neglect of history or of social reference is anathema) it must be noticed that there are strong moves to accommodate structuralism to Marxism. Lucien Goldmann's *genetic structuralism* is the most influential example as he identifies correspondences (homologies) between text and society, locating literature as an expression of particular social movements.[26] It is such developments, and those elements which can successfully resist criticism, which reveal the power and insightfulness of structuralism and can usefully advance our understanding, not simply of literature, but of schooling and social life itself.

NOTES

1 Peters (1981).
2 Three books, widely separated in time and focus, reveal the purposes and range of this human response tradition and its equation with education itself: Richards (1929); Leavis (1972); Mathieson (1975).
3 This 'social' approach to literature is clearly evidenced in Eagleton (1978); Swingewood (1976); Goldmann (1964). Raymond Williams has made a long and distinguished contribution. The best entry to his thought is still *The Long Revolution* (1961); his developing thought can be traced in the essays in *Problems in Materialism and Culture* (1980).
4 A widely influential writer who epitomises such an approach is Marjorie Boulton: *The Anatomy of Poetry* (2nd edition, 1982); *The Anatomy of the Novel* (1975); *The Anatomy of Prose* (1954); *The Anatomy of Drama* (1960); *The Anatomy of Literary Studies* (1980).
   The purpose of this book is to analyse the things that can be analysed and a residue that is wonderful and cannot be explained will always be left (Boulton, 1982, p. 3).
   In sharpest contrast, Terry Eagleton proposes radical revision of what counts as 'literature'; he argues that departments of literature in higher education are Ideological State Apparatuses, and that literary theory is no more than social or political theory, and that it would be far preferable to study 'discursive practices . . . all the way from *Moby Dick* to the Muppet Show' (Eagleton, 1983, pp. 202–7).
5 Different approaches to structuralism and examples of practice can be seen in Culler (1975); Kermode (1979); Lodge (1981); Strickland (1981).
6 David Lodge, 'Oedipuss: or the practice and theory of narrative' in Lodge (1981).
7 The challenge to more familiar approaches to literature – and the intellectual difficulties these alternatives pose can be seen in: Jakobson (1973, pp. 119–29). (David Lodge renders Jakobson more accessible in his *The Modes of Modern Writing*, 1977.) See also Derrida (1978).
8 Josipovici (1979, p. 309).
9 Culler (1975, p. viii).
10 Culler (1975, p. 31).
11 Jakobson and Jones (1970, p. 10).
12 Todorov (1973, pp. 73–103).
13 Rutherford (1977, pp. 43–56).
14 Todorov (1973, p. 73).
15 Culler (1975, p. 31).
16 Julia Kristeva, reported in Culler (1975, p. 258). Kristeva's writing,

like much of post-structuralism, is in the French literary journal *Tel Quel*.

17 Culler (1975, p. 258).

18 Belsey (1980, p. 3).

19 Three useful introductions to the deconstruction movement (embracing such writers as Derrida, Foucault, Bloom, de Man, Hartman and Hillis Miller) are Leitch (1983); Norris (1982); Culler (1983).

20 Barthes (1972b). Roland Barthes was killed in a motor accident in 1980. His work is exhaustively reviewed and sympathetically assessed in Lavers (1982).

21 Culler (1975, p. 242). Such openness to the possibility of an infinity of legitimate interpretation (anything goes?) has had amusing results, particularly among psychoanalytic studies of literature. My own two favourites are the following:

Derrida's agonising over a marginal jotting by Nietzsche, 'I have forgotten my umbrella', asking whether it might contain cryptic significance decipherable only by means of a Freudian or Heideggerian reading; and going on to speculate whether it might not be the case that Nietzsche's entire literary production is of the same undecidable status as the sentence 'I have forgotten my umbrella' (Norris, 1983, p. 21); and Green's speculation:

My hypothesis of Desdemona's love for Cassio as part of the kernel of truth is not complete, however. It must have as its complement another aspect of things, the aspect of which is much more difficult to see and is totally obliterated from the spectator's view. Silent, but effective, the whole mainspring of the tragedy lies here: Othello's desire for Cassio (Green, 1979, p. 107).

22 Bloom (1979, pp. vii and 4) (and note that Roland Barthes claimed that a text 'contains, finally, no heart, no kernel, no secret, no irreducible principle, nothing except the infinity of its own envelopes – which envelop nothing other than the unity of its own surfaces'; quoted in Culler, 1975, p. 259).

23 Rutherford (1977, p. 50).

24 Strickland (1981, pp. 15–26).

25 Watson (1978, Chapter 2). George Watson is a severe, even contemptuous, critic of structuralism:

The structural interest in human conviction can only be reductive in the end. Nobody who is seriously concerned with the truth and falsehood of religious and other commitments should be *primarily* concerned with the patterns and symmetries they form . . . structuralism was a playground, and in the end nothing better than that (pp. 33–4).

26 Goldmann (1964). Lucien Goldmann traces the structural relationship between the thought of Pascal and Racine and a social group, the *noblesse de robe* of seventeenth-century France.

7 Structuralism and Education

At first sight, structuralism might appear to have little to offer to teachers. Its insistence on systems, wholes, relationships, together with the apparent devaluation of the individual in its 'decentring of the subject', all run counter to the child-centred, individualistic, humanistic assumptions of most teachers. Add to that structuralism's marked preference for theory and abstraction, and the contrast with teachers' preference for action and practice becomes even more obvious. Structuralist approaches seem less appealing than those which study what is familiar, concrete, visible; matters of common-sense experience and practical action which are 'human' and 'natural'. Thus, child-studies are more congenial than studies of social context (John and Mary and their vivid presence are more urgently demanding than 'capitalism' or 'democracy'). Acceptance of common-sense notions of 'intelligence' or 'maladjustment' are preferred to study of how such categories are socially constructed (John is patently dim and difficult, Mary bright and sensible when faced with the obvious tasks of school). And explanations of schools and classrooms which centre on distant structural and historical factors are discounted in favour of those which are local, personal, and immediately, obviously, present. (Talk of working-class values, or the historical grip of the grammar school curriculum, doesn't seem to solve how to occupy John today, at *this* moment.) In the face of the pressing demands of school and classroom, it is not surprising that teachers accord low priority to modes of understanding which seem to be at some remove from practice.

But structural approaches can be of immense benefit to teachers in their understanding and practice of education. We have seen in Chapter 3 how the structuralist theories of Piaget have influenced the thought and classroom action of teachers. Most teachers accept, with little questioning, the structuralist model of intellectual development he proposes. They experience few problems in accommodating the theory to their practice. Indeed, for most primary teachers (certainly for almost all infant teachers) it both underpins and directs their classroom practice as they readily make links between individual and structure. These links may not be quite so formally expressed as, 'John is still at the stage of concrete operations, therefore . . .', but the *form* of assumption is similar: children of this age can/cannot do that. So, in the area of what I call structures of thought, the application of structuralism to education has been a success story, even if that structuralist success has been an unacknowledged one.

In this chapter I shall identify three other structuralist approaches to education which, in different ways, have had increasing impact on the theory and practice of schooling. I call them conventional structuralism, process structuralism, and Bernstein's structuralism. I have chosen critically to analyse Bernstein's structuralism in much greater detail than either conventional or process structuralism. This is not because I value his work less than the other two approaches, but for four major reasons: first, because he exemplifies many of the features of European structuralism discussed in preceding chapters; second, because I believe most readers will be unfamiliar with the actual nature and weaknesses of Bernstein's theorising (in spite of his being well known to teachers); third, because my detailed critique of Bernstein will stand for criticism of this type of structuralism in general; and fourth, because Bernstein is without doubt one of the most exciting and intellectually demanding writers that any student of education will encounter. Like Levi-Strauss, he gives his readers (to mix metaphors) a bumpy, frustrating and puzzling ride, but never a dull one.

I shall conclude the chapter by suggesting how certain structuralist concepts can illuminate practice and thus help to change it. This will prepare the way for my method of structural analysis developed in Chapter 8.

Conventional Structuralism

I have already hinted at this approach in the early pages of Chapter 4. Many of its features are familiar and uncontroversial, reflected in the common-sense assumptions of teachers. It is far distanced from the European, theoretical forms of structuralism we have encountered earlier. Thus, in everyday conversation, we speak of 'the local education authority (the LEA)', 'the education system', 'the school', 'parents', 'pupils', as if they were 'wholes' about which generalisations can be made. We assume the existence and power of these 'wholes', accepting that they direct or influence the behaviour of those individuals who are included in the categories. Such terms are part of our everyday language. Social life would be impossible without them. We speak and act *as if* (key words!) such collectivities have being and real significance. Similarly, we take for granted that something we call 'society' influences or directs schooling.

These kinds of common-sense, everyday assumptions become formalised into what can be called conventional (or sociological) structuralism. In this the links between society and the education system become more tightly defined, more deterministic ('School reflects society'). At the same time there is much confidence about the existence and measurability of groups and group characteristics. Social class, sex, race, religion, age, become major taken-for-granted categories for investigation, each group yielding a wealth of empirical data. In the collection and analysis of such data, the methods and assumptions of science are both adopted and promoted: the objectivity of social phenomena, the existence of laws or rules which govern or guide behaviour, and the use of the empirical method to ascertain (almost) value-free truths. This kind of structuralism has an apparent simplicity about it. Social structure is like the skeleton of a body: observable, measurable, clearly functional. It is 'there' in a very obvious sense. But the approach is neither homogeneous nor uncontroversial as can be readily grasped through three examples of its practice.

First, an example of conventional structuralism which has had an undeniably great impact on education and, even more directly, on every British reader of this book. Two decades ago, the Robbins Report on Higher Education (Department of Education and Science, 1963) commissioned the collection of a huge amount of statistical evidence, much of it relating to working-class under-achievement in education. What was shown clearly was the existence of a 'pool of ability' both wider and deeper than had previously been suspected. To give only one example: of those children born to manual-class parents in 1940–1, only 3% of boys and 1% of girls undertook full-time degree courses (and of those whose IQ was 115–129, only 8% took degree level courses when in fact all were intellectually capable of doing so). As a direct result of the Robbins Report's recommendations that this pool ability should be more effectively tapped and utilised, a quite staggering expansion of higher education took place in the second half of the

1960s. The polytechnic system was created, the university system was vastly expanded, and teacher education itself briefly grew to unthought-of dimensions. At the time of publication of the Robbins Report there were 216,000 students in full-time higher education; in 1980–1 the figure was over 467,000. Within these figures, teacher education had expanded from 55,000 in 1962 to 113,000 in 1971 (falling to 27,000 in 1981). The Robbins Report adopted a conventional structuralist approach to higher education; groups and systems rather than individuals were its focus of attention. The structural consequences of the Report (and, hence, consequences for individuals) were striking in the extreme as greatly increased numbers of students experienced higher education. And its basic principle (only recently rejected by the New Conservatism) that anyone qualified was entitled to a place in higher education can be seen as both echoing and significantly contributing to the structure of feeling of optimism and expansion that characterised the 1960s.

The second example is also familiar but more controversial. It is that kind of structuralism proposed by Emile Durkheim and currently exemplified in the work of A. H. Halsey. Heavily committed to empirical investigation, it also has a strong interest in theory and sees schooling as an instrument of cultural reproduction. Thus education reflects, maintains and reproduces the society in which it is set. Schooling acts as an agent of society, interacting with other social institutions (family, religion, media, and so on) to maintain existing social systems, particularly social class stratification. Halsey's work provides excellent examples of such structuralism in the Durkheim tradition with its fairly benign view of the relations between education and society. Nonetheless, although Halsey is committed to the *liberal ideology* (education is valuable in itself and is a beneficial instrument of social change), all his writings, whether on the Educational Priority Area schemes he directed consequent on the Plowden Report, or on social mobility in modern Britain, demonstrate clearly both the existence of social inequalities and the contribution of the education system in maintaining them.[1] The chance of entry to universities for a working-class child, for example, remains what it was in the 1930s (or is even lower). Education functions to reproduce existing inequalities of income, status and power. This is not the conscious intention of teachers and others involved in the education system, indeed, their intentions may be consciously egalitarian, but the structures in which they are embedded ensure such inegalitarian outcomes and so maintain themselves.

A third example of conventional structuralism dismisses the relative optimism of Durkheim and Halsey, who do allow for some amelioration of social inequality, particularly through education. Marxist versions of conventional structuralism are heavily deterministic: education is in the *grip* of society. More particularly, it is the grip of economic forces which comprise the *base* of society. Base determines *superstructure* (education, politics, religion, and so on). Thus education is simply one of the instruments by which inequalities ('relations of production') are maintained. We saw in Chapter 4 that recent Marxists, notably Louis Althusser, have attempted to loosen the structural chains of economic determinism by allowing the education system a good deal of independence. In spite of such revisionism, Marxist analyses of education tie educational origins, purposes and functions to the economic structure of society. Bowles' and Gintis' *Schooling in Capitalist America*[2] is notorious for such economic determinism. In their account schooling can be seen to mirror the social relationships of factory life under capitalism. As a consequence it produces the types of labour force required: subordinate, conforming workers and self-controlled, initiatory managers. The economic structuring of education is omnipresent, ominous and oppressive. This type of 'correspondence theory' lays itself open to criticism for its crude over-simplifications and its neglect of disconfirming realities (particularly and peculiarly, industrial conflict).

In a more interesting version of Marxist structuralism, Kevin Harris attempts to show how structures of thought are produced by the conditions of capitalist society such that:

> . . . education is not a revelation of truth . . . an initiation . . . into liberation of the mind from ignorance or the creation of free man.

Rather, education in capitalist liberal democracies 'atrophies the capacity of people to think of alternatives'.[3]

Harris argues that schooling actually 'transmits knowledge that distorts people's view of the world' and offers a 'structured misrepresentation of reality' which 'promotes false consciousness'. These are grave charges, far removed from Halsey's or the Robbins Report's more optimistic structuralism. Harris asserts that capitalist structures pervade and pervert schooling, working through the curriculum to produce in learners a consciousness that accepts and hence maintains the economic inequalities on which capitalism is based. School knowledge acts as 'a perception altering drug', which distorts the consciousness of pupils and teachers alike. But Harris' fiercely applied economic structuralism founders on its own neatness and a mere return to Bowles and Gintis:

> . . . the conduct and process of education in a capitalist society corresponds neatly with the conduct and process of the workplace.[4]

Here, much is made of structural characteristics: knowledge mediated through controllers, stratified lines of authority, the social and technical fragmentation of learning, external motivation and so on. The complexity of classroom relationships is submerged by a concern to fit them to all-encompassing Marxist theory. Both these accounts represent hard-line Marxism where the level of the discussion and the drive of the argument are ill-received by most teachers whose preference is for more local, less deterministic analyses. The furore which greeted the publication of the Open University's *Schooling and Capitalism*[5] was evidence of the mistrust of teachers of what looks to them like conspiracy theory or denial of autonomy. Few teachers enjoy versions of schooling which cast them and their pupils as little more than puppets in the hands of distant, structural puppet-masters whose control of action, through economic forces, is absolute. Harris' claims that 'the material conditions of existing social relations . . . determine what shall be transmitted and how', and his assertion that 'Education . . . is controlled by the ruling class, the capitalists, to serve their own interests', fall on deaf ears of teachers faced with the multiple demands and realities of actual classrooms. Although Marxism dismisses the other forms of structuralism discussed elsewhere in this book, its own structuralism is total. And as its version is heavily critical of the liberal, humanistic ideology which informs education in the West, it is not surprising that the Open University material and Harris' book encountered such hostile receptions.

Process Structuralism

The term process structuralism refers to those accounts which focus on school and classroom processes which evidence and reproduce structures. Like conventional structuralism it is heterogeneous but possesses common characteristics. Thus, although there is great variety, each study is based on accounts of small-group interaction. Case studies using anthropological, ethnographic methods characterise the approach. Although the various analyses are usually vivid and highly readable, detailing as they do participants' accounts or actions, nonetheless their drive is to show how social life and social categories are *constructed* not *given*. The approach seeks to identify those structural forces, whether material or mental, which shape and influence individual behaviour, and which are themselves the product of everyday human action. A few examples show how the method differs both from conventional structuralism and empiricism.

We have already encountered in Chapter 5 Ronald King's study of three infant schools, *All Things Bright and Beautiful?*[6] Through close observation of the actual behaviour of infant teachers, King identifies a structure of beliefs which informs and guides their actions. Its four components (developmentalism, individualism, play as learning, and a belief in childhood innocence) act powerfully to ensure that her actual classroom experience confirms the way the teacher 'sees' her children. In Chapter 5 this ideology was interpreted as a structure of feeling: the beliefs produce and explain actual outcomes. Although King's work might seem a far cry from Raymond Williams' discussions of how major authors transform the evaluative climates of their times, nonetheless it is an impressive piece of process structuralism. It clearly shows how, *through action*, typifications or categories ('good pupil', 'bright', 'bouncy', 'slow', 'nice') are created and maintained. Conventionally identified structures such as capitalism or liberalism are far distant from this closely-focused process study.

In marked contrast is Willis' research into 'why do working-class kids get working-class jobs?' as he vividly portrays how twelve teenage 'lads' penetratingly grasp the nature of the social structure in which they find themselves. In what Willis sees as rational and positive acts, the lads actively construct their own realities, drawing on lower working-class, factory-floor values as a resource to sustain their beliefs and behaviour. They see they are destined for manual jobs, they perceive themselves as school failures; they therefore reject school conformity as pointless: why *should* they submit to 'them'? Yet for all their apparent creativity in their linguistic and behavioural rejection of conformism, Willis shows the lads are caught in a social structure which itself produces their opposition. He argues that the system that is capitalism creates the lads' responses. For all their 'freedom' and spontaneity, the most significant shaper and explainer of their beliefs and actions are the relationships of the social structure within which they are contained. Willis' account is unremittingly Marxist:

> The whole nature of Western Capitalism is also such that classes are structured and persistent so that even relatively high rates of individual mobility make no difference to the existence or position of the working class.[7]

Here is conventional structuralism in pure form: distanced, Olympian, with the individual nowhere in sight. But Willis' vital contribution is to show the inter-personal dynamics, the processes of those structures. His clear identification of the minute-to-minute construction of reality in the lived experience of his lads suggests how that process creates and maintains both identity and structure.

Although its focus and style are somewhat different, an equally impressive example of Marxist process structuralism is Sharp and Green's account of how social control is exercised through the daily experiences of pupils and teachers in a progressive primary school.[8] They show how self-fulfilling prophecies arise and are confirmed in material conditions which impose a structure of constraints on teachers' actions. Although they are much concerned, like King, with infant teachers' ideologies, they produce, for Marxists, a curiously deficient account of how those ideologies relate to and are grounded in the material structures of capitalism.

The process structuralism of King, Willis and Sharp and Green hinges on research undertaken on pupils in 'normal' schools. Recently there has been increasing concentration on the processes of 'special education': the ways in which certain pupils are classified and treated as being, in Warnock's phrase, 'children with special needs'. The very titles of papers and books identify the assumptions and argument of this process structuralism: 'The social construction of the ESN(M) child'; *Special Education and Social Control: Invisible Disasters.*[9] In such research we find a clear rejection of any internal essence ('maladjustment', 'autism', 'poor intelligence') and a concentration on the *relationships of the system* within which children categorised as 'special' are set: the world of special education itself. The approach stresses that the really important features of special education and its pupils are its own social processes and structures within the social structure which contain them. As such it plays down any notion of 'given', 'natural', or inner conditions which are familiar to and taken for granted by many teachers. Rather, it is through these processes and these structures, argue the process structuralists (notably Sally Tomlinson and Julienne Ford), that the special child is produced, not by virtue of any objective, inner state. As Squibb puts it:

> . . . there is a structuralist imperative to look for the processes which produce the (special) categories rather than to assume that the category arises immaculately from the inner qualities or essence of the child.[10]

Teachers faced with what they see as a dyslexic, maladjusted, or educationally subnormal child are often impatient with or dismissive of such an approach. But this powerful structuralist argument and its supporting evidence cannot be ignored in its requirement that research should focus on the *system* rather than the individual child or the 'thing' (educational subnormality). Such focus shows that 'inferior' groups in society are over-represented in certain categories of special education. Few middle-class children, for example, are classified as ESN(M); children from lower social class homes (and blacks) predominate.

As Sally Tomlinson remarks:

> The middle and upper classes in the late twentieth century simply do not allow, or need their children to be socially constructed as ESN(M).[11]

The inference, plainly, is that special education is a structural element which helps maintain inequality and privilege by convincing some children that they are in fact inferior. On this account, special education is a form of stigmatisation to legitimate existing structures. This inference is too strong for most teachers to take, containing as it does a massive 'decentring of the subject' as it reduces the undoubted goodwill of teachers to insignificance beside the structure-maintaining function of special education. Nonetheless process structuralism undoubtedly reveals the machinery and experience through which pupils become categorised. This level of analysis takes two forms. First, it identifies the large increase over the years in the number of pupils categorised as being in special need and links such growth with the number of adults working in the special education field and the substantial developments that have taken place in the career structure of teachers of pupils with special needs. The contributions of these professionals, psychologists, teachers, heads, doctors, social workers, psychiatrists, assessment centre staff, educational welfare officers and others are described ironically as 'smooth team-work' which creates the child with special needs. The second form of analysis closely examines this 'teamwork' by means of detailed observation of the classification process of actual children. Here, studies of case conferences and interviews with those involved in the classification procedures are characterised by such statements as:

> The category of ESN(M) is socially constructed by the decisions and beliefs of professional people.[12]

> Direct observation would suggest that even if there were no consistent prejudice at work, heads and teachers can hardly be trusted to be impartial.[13]

> The sum of all these honest endeavours is far greater than the total of its parts. The processes which envelop these children lay claim to all the virtuous characteristics described immediately above (scrupulous-ness, impartiality, a sense of accountability) through their apparent espousal of the intentions of the people who service the processes. Unfortunately the models which are available for these people to use . . . contrive with the statutory, institutional and social restraints operating upon the field to deflect the efforts into a product which is arbitrary and discriminatory in the pejorative sense of that word.[14]

The process structuralism in such comments is evident: the system *itself* produces the special child together with the 'appropriate' social and individual responses to him or her. Struc-ture dominates, even though attitudes and treatments of the special child may be massively informed by goodwill. Researchers point to the fact that identification and treatment of special needs children is based on the 'medical model', an approach to subnor-mality based on the *individual pupil* who is held to possess identifiable, objective, measurable, intrinsic traits, rather than upon the *system* within which the individual is embedded. This individual-based approach is held to be inadequate to the under-standing or treatment of special needs. In the words of Julienne Ford, its inadequacy lies in its failure:

> . . . to meet satisfactorily the needs of a situation dominated by an essentially administrative response, to a series of socially determined problems.[15]

And in a discussion of her research into referral decisions in fifteen comprehensives Ford stresses the structural imperative:

We are observing the social and subjective determinants of a model which is ostensibly objective . . . It is difficult to escape the conclusion that the organisation of the secondary schools, along with their 'public' and 'hidden' curriculum, inevitably determines and defines maladjustment in some pupils who might be treated quite differently in another environment and ethos.[16]

If two central weaknesses of conventional structuralism lie in its assumption of the taken-for-granted objectivity of social phenomena (*reification*), and its preference for social 'laws' which have the force of scientific laws, then process structuralism possesses corresponding major flaws. Both are illustrated in the examples above: first, the tendency to slide into relativity (no objectivity exists), and second, the over-commitment to the *social* construction of reality as if nature did not limit that reality.

The Structuralism of Basil Bernstein

Professor Bernstein has been, for two decades, the best-known British sociologist of education. His theorising, particularly about language and curriculum, has been a central focus in teacher education. However ill-understood, his concepts have become a necessary element in any discussion of schooling. To enquire into pupil success or failure without taking Bernstein into account is impossible. What has rarely been acknowledged however (Atkinson (1981) is a notable exception) is that Bernstein is a structuralist with all the characteristics of European structuralism and as such considerably removed from other British sociologists of education. He is far closer to Levi-Strauss than to Anglo-Saxon empiricism, but it is a remarkable testament to his imaginative structuralism that he exercises so powerful an influence over teachers' consciousness in spite of his abstract and difficult writing style.

Bernstein's endeavour has always been remarkably single-minded and consistent. From his first paper in 1958 for over a quarter of a century he has explored the sources of working-class pupils' under-attainment in schools by seeking the mechanisms by which culture and society, acting on and through individual action and consciousness, manifests and reproduces itself. Such mechanisms include the familiar sociological concerns of social class relationships, language, family structures, socialisation processes, curriculum. But they also include his own uniquely structuralist contribution: to establish the *codes* which govern language, consciousness, meaning and curriculum, society itself. And, as we shall see, it is this latter concern with codes which has always dominated and typified Bernstein's work. I shall first briefly identify his *conventional structuralism* and then move to a discussion and critique of his own distinctive structuralism.

Bernstein's conventional structuralism

In this, Bernstein resembles other sociologists and the examples discussed earlier in this chapter. His concern is not simply to link language, curriculum or childrearing-practices with social structure but to root them in it. Here, social structure *causes* language or socialisation procedures. Each item of Bernstein's writings invariably begins and ends with such a claim: the origin of behaviour and experience is social structure and social relationships (that is, social class). Some examples clearly demonstrate the continuity of Bernstein's thought within this conventional, familiar sociological mode of explanation. Page references are from sources given in Note 17, page 135, italics are mine.

1958   The middle-class child is capable of responding to, manipulating and understanding language . . . *as a result of his class environment* . . . *Because of the different structuring of the working-class environment* the working-class child . . . is limited to expressive symbolism and a public language (p. 37).

1960   It is proposed that the two distinct forms of language use arise *because of* the organisation of the two social strata (p. 61).

1962   One of the tasks of the sociologist's work is to *seek the social origins* of particular linguistic forms . . . *social structure transforms* language possibility into a specific code (p. 76).

1965   . . . the form of the social relationship, or more generally, *the social structure generates distinctive linguistic forms or codes* . . . Every time the child speaks or listens the social structure of which he is a part is reinforced in him and his social identity is constrained (pp. 122–4).

1971   These two codes, elaborated and restricted, are *generated by a particular form of social relation.* Indeed they are likely to be a *realisation of different social structures* (p. 146).

1973   A major aim of the research has been to try and understand the *basic social controls on the form and content of symbolic orders* transmitted initially in the family and in the process of education (p. 237).

1975   The thesis . . . asserts categorically (and it has always done this) that *there is a causal relationship between the structure of social relationships and the structure of communication* (p. 30).

1977   Class is conceived as the fundamental *dominant cultural category* . . . it is the basic classification *which creates the social relationships of production* . . . Thus variations in the codes of education and production are *different historical realisations of the dominant cultural category* (p. 175).

1982   Class relations generate, distribute, reproduce and legitimate distinctive forms of communication, which transmit dominating and dominated codes . . . codes are *culturally determined positioning devices* (pp. 304–5).

Here we can see clearly the first, utterly consistent feature of Bernstein's structuralist project: social class structure controls experience. He is clearly preoccupied with what he refers to as 'the grim consequences of class relationships' (1975, p. 1). In this his structuralism is recognisably related to the mainstream of British and American sociology of education. But right from the start of his writing can be seen his own particular brand of structuralism which sets him apart from the Anglo-Saxon tradition and which links him strongly to European traditions of thought.

Bernstein's structuralism: codes, classification and framing

In his concern to develop a theory of educational transmissions, analysing changes in forms of social control and their consequences for schooling, Bernstein produces his own, distinctive set of structuralist concepts. His fascination with the notions of *code*, *classification* and *framing* and his repeated exploration and expansion of them show they are more central to his thought than conventional structuralism. They become his structuralist tools to analyse and explain the links between social class and educational experience. Indeed, for Bernstein, *code, classification* and *framing* take increasing force as the regulators of, and linkages between, structure and individual, social relationships and language. Thus, if his first assumption is that social structure regulates and causes speech or behaviour, then his second is that the crucial regulation or causation is effected by codes, classification and framing. Language or action in classrooms is governed and produced by codes. In short, Bernstein offers a conceptual scheme in which the concepts direct behaviour. The structuralist notions of code, classification and framing *become* the originators and enforcers of individual and social action. So mesmerised is Bernstein by his structuralist concepts that they take precedence over all other forms of explanations, looming larger than the social structures they reproduce. For all his stress on social class structure and his attempt in recent years to accommodate Marxism, Bernstein's writing demonstrates his progressive enmeshment with, expansion of, and domination by, his structuralist concepts. In his search for a theory to explain how society (as structure, power and control) through certain agencies (social class, family, school) reproduces itself through individuals (as language, identity, consciousness), his crucial determinants are code, classification and frame.

Bernstein remarks, 'Occasionally, a concept is useful and can take endless exploration' (1971, p. 2). His key concepts have certainly experienced that as he has pursued his interest in the processes of cultural transmission. His earliest (1958) paper hints at what is to come with its quickly abandoned 'structure-content' concepts as the basis of different orders of perception arising from 'public' or 'formal' language. Two following papers (1959, 1960) examine how 'social structure becomes part of individual experience' (p. 54) through two different *modes* (note, not yet *codes*) of speech. Public language, for example, 'powerfully reinforces the initially socially induced preference' for providing social rather than individual symbols (p. 47). In 1962 *modes* give way to *codes* and Bernstein makes explicit his quest for a theory of social learning which will link social structure, language use and individual behaviour. His own particular brand of structuralism makes its first formally stated appearance in the second half of the following sentence (my italics; note that the first half of the sentence is conventional structuralism):

> . . . social structure transforms language possibility into *a specific code which elicits, generalizes and reinforces those relationships necessary for its continuance* (p. 76).

Here, social structure is dominant ('transforms'), but note the three active verbs ('elicits, generalizes and reinforces') which prefigure the power *code* will assume as Bernstein develops it.

From now on Bernstein's attention is centred on 'codes' and the enlarged application of that concept characterises all his writing. His interest in *language codes* (elaborated–restricted) is succeeded by *curriculum codes* and then by a concept of code which is all-inclusive, embracing *meanings, realisations, contexts* and *social class* itself. First consider some examples which demonstrate the growing imperialism of *code* applied to language.

1962 . . . restricted and elaborated codes *will establish* different kinds of control . . . which establish the patterns of orientation, association and organization (p. 81).

1965 A change of code involves changes in the *means* whereby social identity and reality are created (p. 137).

1969 . . . the deep structure of communication is *controlled by* a restricted code . . . (or) an elaborated code (p. 198).

1971(a) I am suggesting that if we look into the work relationships of (a) particular group, its community relationships, its family role systems, it is reasonable to argue that *the genes of social class may well be carried* less through a genetic code but far more *through a communication code* that social class itself promotes (p. 143).

A social role can then be considered as a complex *coding activity controlling both the creation and organisation of specific meanings* and the conditions for their transmission and reception (pp. 144–5).

1971(a) Linguistic codes are *basic controls on the transmission of a culture or subculture and are the creators of social identity* (p. 164).

1971(b) Codes symbolize the form of the social relationship, regulate the nature of the speech encounters, and *create for the speakers different orders of relevance and relation* (p. 174).

In 1971 Bernstein extended his theory of codes from sociolinguistics to the sociology of knowledge (i.e. from language to curriculum). In his analysis of the school curriculum he now begins to speak of 'educational knowledge codes' as 'Underlying principles which shape curriculum, pedagogy and evaluation' (p. 203). He also introduces two new concepts, *classification* and *framing*, which, he claims, would aid his endeavour:

. . . to understand the interrelationships between symbolic orders, form of social organisation and the shaping of experience in terms of codes (p. 202).

His structuralism becomes even more pronounced in its exploitation of the key structuralist concept of *relationships* expressed (via classification and frame) as *boundary strength*. Classification is taken to refer to degree of boundary maintenance between (curriculum) contents; frame refers to the degree of control teacher and pupil possess over the selection, organisation, pacing and timing of the knowledge transmitted and received in the pedagogical relationship. Using these two new concepts Bernstein now identifies two 'curriculum codes' (integrated code, collection code) whose distinctiveness is given by strength of classification and frame (that is, by strength of boundary maintenance). Collection codes are strongly classified and framed, integrated codes have weak boundary maintenance between school subjects and allow greater control to pupils (that is, weak classification and framing).

Bernstein's structuralism (codes determine perception, experience and identity; they reproduce culture, social structure) is evidenced throughout. Codes are all-powerful:

> The deep structure of the specialized type of collection code is strong boundary maintenance *creating control from within through the formation of specific identities* (p. 96).

> The European and English forms of the collection code may provide for those who go beyond the novitiate stage, order, identity and commitment (p. 100).

> . . . collection codes *increase the discretion of teachers* . . . integrated codes *will reduce the discretion of teachers* (p. 101).

> With the collection code . . . only the elite have access to the deep structure, and therefore *access to the experiential knowledge that new realities are possible* (p. 102).

> This change of code involves fundamental changes in the classification and framing of knowledge *and so changes in the structure and distribution of power and in principles of control* (p. 106).

Although initially Bernstein restricts application of classification and framing to curriculum (subject boundaries and teacher/pupil control over what is taught and how), the concepts undergo, as does code, rapid expansion in this 1971 paper and in his 1973 paper on visible and invisible pedagogies. In the latter paper, the analysis is conducted almost entirely in terms of classification and framing, but always, in this exploration of school and family socialisation of young children, his concern is to persuade the reader of the existence of educational knowledge codes which are the crucial regulators of experience and the means by which social reproduction is effected.

It is in the 1973 paper that the all-inclusive properties and powers of *code* are made manifest:

> . . . a change in code (is) a change in the principles of relation and evaluation whether these are principles of knowledge, of social relationships, of practices, of property, of identity (p. 145).

The centrality of *code* as both concept and cause is made clear:

> Thus a shift from invisible to visible pedagogies in one phrase is a change in code (p. 145).

> . . . the family (of new middle-class children) contains both codes – the code *which creates the manifestation of the person* and the *code which creates private properties* (p. 145).

Even though Bernstein roots codes in class structures and insists that 'to change the code controlling transmission involves changing the culture and its basis in privatised class relationships' (p. 145), nonetheless he concludes his paper with a clear indication of the power of codes:

> . . . the move to weak classification and frames (i.e. integrated codes) has the *potential* of reducing insulations in mental structures and social structures (p. 146).

On this account, *codes* can affect both structures of thought and structures of society. Indeed, throughout all Bernstein's writing the power he attributes to codes is quite extraordinary. His language is remarkably active. His codes 'generate', 'permit', 'weaken', 'require', 'create', 'make possible', 'enable', 'regulate', 'determine', 'release', 'co-ordinate', 'shape' and perform other actions. Their causal nature is marked in the extreme. Codes may arise from forms of social relationship, but they rapidly attain an autonomy and a causal power all of their own. Over and over in Bernstein's explanations, codes, classification and framing take over from social structure and become the springs of action. In 1975 he powerfully re-emphasises his structuralist concern for *relationships* and structures of thought:

> I believe that the structure of socialisation is not a set of roles but classification and framing relationships. It is these, I think, that shape

the mental structures, by establishing coding procedures which are predicated upon distinctive rules (p. 11).

By 1977 Bernstein is redefining codes both as prime movers and as structures of thought. They are:

> . . . the basic message structures of the school (p. 177).

> . . . the fundamental principles which create the everyday activity (p. 176).

> . . . a code is a regulative principle, tacitly acquired, which integrates relevant meanings, the form of their realization and their evolving contexts (p. 180).

The expansion of the concept and its application also continue as he moves on to speak of 'dominating and dominated codes' and of 'codes of production' (p. 181).

As ever, the structure of the argument is clear: the dominant cultural category (class) is the origin of power and control relations and reproduces those relationships through codes. But codes are Bernstein's major interest and the history of capitalism, from entrepreneurial to corporate, is encompassed within his 'codes of production' as he asserts the general correspondence 'between the dominant education code *collection* and the dominant code of production' (p. 185).

By 1982 Bernstein's own brand of structuralism has come to full fruition in his 'Codes, modalities and the process of cultural reproduction: a model'. Still preoccupied with the problem of how society, through individuals, reproduces itself, his thesis is that:

> . . . class relations generate, distribute, reproduce and legitimate, distinctive forms of communication, which transmit dominating and dominated codes: and that subjects (i.e. individuals) are differentially positioned by these codes in the process of their acquisition (pp. 304–5).

Although the codes are 'class regulated', Bernstein's concentration is upon the work they do; they:

> . . . position subjects with respect to dominating and dominated form of communication *and* to the relationships between them. Ideology is constituted through and in, such positioning (p. 305).

Code is now defined as:

> a regulative principle, tacitly acquired, which selects and integrates . . . meanings, realisations, contexts (p. 306).

Here *code* echoes Levi-Strauss' pursuit of unconscious structures of mind. It is clearly structuralist, as too is Bernstein's stress on *relationships* not utterances or contexts:

> . . . code is a regulator of the relationships *between* contexts and, through that relationship, a regulator of the relationships *within* contexts. What counts as context depends not upon relationships *within* but *relationships between* contexts (p. 306).

This concern for *relationships* is a paradigm example of structuralist thought. So, too, is the work Bernstein gives to *code*, for this device *selects* and *integrates* meanings, realisations, contexts; *regulates* relations between contexts; *generates* principles for distinguishing between contexts; and *generates* principles for the *creation and production* of specialised relationships within a context (p. 306). Equally clear is Bernstein's structuralist stress on *transformations*: to write specific codes he seeks to show the means:

> . . . whereby it is possible to perform the following transformations:
> (1) class relations and positioning (via power and control)
> (2) positioning and codes
> (3) codes and communication.
> If such transformations can be accomplished then the invisible can be recovered from the visible (p. 307).

This very high level of abstraction of Bernstein's writing is typical of European structuralism and is unfamiliar to most British or American students of education. The homely example he gives may help us to grasp his intentions more clearly. He reports an enquiry carried out by the Sociological Research Unit into how children classify. Sixty children were presented with coloured pictures of food (bread, cheese, fish fingers, and so on) and asked to group them as they liked. Working-class children produced categories more tied to direct experience than middle-class children. They grouped more on the basis of 'it's what we eat at home', 'what Mum makes', than middle-class children who were more likely to volunteer 'these came from the sea', 'these all have butter in them' (pages 308–9). Bernstein calls these two classifications 'elaborated and restricted coding orientations to meanings'. His endeavour is to show how these thought-styles relate to and emerge from a material (that is, social class) context. He suggests the more specific and local the base, the more restricted the coding orientation. His 1982 paper becomes an attempt to develop a model showing how 'the distribution of power and principles of control' regulate such realisations of orientation to meaning (to show how such everyday classifications emerge from social structure). But, as always, in this structuralism, *code* predominates. The model is:

> . . . for generating codes regulating the class production of physical resources and class reproduction and production of discursive resources (p. 312).

Note the power of codes here: they regulate not simply education or communication (discursive resources) but 'class production of physical resources' as well! For all his insistence on social structure, for Bernstein it is his *codes* which do the work. And his long march through classification and framing produces a surprisingly precise method of identifying codes which perform that work of governing education, communication and economic relationships. It is worth giving his finding in full, for it exemplifies his structuralism:

> We can now write specific codes regulating the reproduction/production of physical and discursive resources in terms of orientation to meanings and their realisations, created by specialised interactional practices constituting communicative contexts. Codes can be specified by the following formula
>
> $$\frac{O}{(\pm)C\ F(\pm)^{i/e}}$$
>
> Where
> O   refers to the orientation to meanings elaborated/restricted (privileged/privileging referential relations)
> C   refers to the principle of classification
> F   refers to the principle of framing
> $(\pm)$ refers to the values of C & F with respect to strength (strong/weak)
> i/e i refers to the *internal* values of F *within* a communicative context for example, family, school and work
>   e refers to the *external* values of F, that is the regulation on communicative relations *between* communicative contexts for example, family/community and school, school and work (pp. 331–2).

Before moving to a necessary critique, it is now possible to summarise the nature of Bernstein's structuralism. It has both the surface features of European structuralism and its deep structure (see Chapters 1 and 2). Thus it is highly abstract; it employs the familiar structuralist notions of *codes, relationships, transformations*; and it creates its own structuralist concepts (*classification* and *framing*). It is unafraid of shifts into imaginative, sonorous, significance-loaded, gnomic utterances ('the subject is established by the silence through which power speaks') which are elusive and illusive, mythic, poetic, dense, obscure. Throughout the enduring preoccupation with *codes*, whether of language, curriculum, socialisation or cultural reproduction, Bernstein's work is characterised by the duality of concepts which have the form of structural *binary oppositions* (elaborated/restricted, open/closed, implicit/explicit, intimacy/distance, visible/invisible, positional/personal, collection/integrated, instrumental/expressive, mechanical/organic, stratified/differentiated, purity/mixture, classification/frame, power/control). It has the sheer scale and ambition of Levi-Strauss in its construction of a grand theory of all-encompassing codes, and has structuralism's confident claim to scientific precision ('codes can be specified by the following formula . . .') in identifying causal factors. Those causal factors are *codes*, which undergo almost infinite application and expansion, becoming the sources and springs of human action as they variously 'generate', 'transform', 'reproduce', 'create', 'move', 'govern', 'integrate', etc. Then, too, there is the structuralist preoccupation with language. Although Bernstein returns again and again to the familiar sociological claim that social structure is the root and determiner of human action, he invariably converts this assertion into a structuralism in which abstract rules, structures of mind (i.e. codes, classification, framing) are both the focus of attention and the significant explainers of action.[18] His bewitchment by language ensures he always returns to codes in spite of his attempts to harness his scheme to the material world. There is the decentring of the subject, as human action becomes the result of its containing system ('class codes . . . by which and through which subjects are selectively created, positioned and oppositioned', page 336). Finally, Bernstein's writing, like European structuralism, has become impenetrable to the layman. Even the most academically inclined British or American teacher finds his latest paper unfamiliar and difficult:

Codes are transformations with specific semiotic principles/grammars of the relations and realisations of categories, where category relations represent the paradigmatic and realisations represent the syntagmatic (p. 336).

This single sentence from the conclusion of his 1982 paper has all major hallmarks of structuralist thought: the sentence could have emerged from Paris in the 1960s – and would have been entirely at home there.

These characteristics suggest the weaknesses which inhere in Bernstein's work. Although he must be applauded for ensuring that language and curriculum have become central concerns for the study of education, nonetheless his structuralism contains faults which, for all its imaginative power, disable the theory of codes. The criticisms can be briefly stated.

1   Concept enlargement and elasticity

The all-encompassing expansion of the basic concepts (code, classification, framing) makes them slippery and elusive; language, knowledge, education, social class and even physical resources come under their power. Bernstein presses *code* into service to produce a universal explanatory scheme. In so doing, with the constant shifts of definition, the notion of *code* becomes so elastic that it loses credibility. That which explains everything explains nothing.

2   The tautological nature of the scheme

With the introduction of *classification* and *framing*, Bernstein produces not an explanatory scheme but a series of definitions and redefinitions. His crucial 1971 and 1982 papers are shot through with tautologies masquerading as logical or causal connections. Bernstein defines both classification and framing in terms of boundary relations (classification = relations between categories, or boundary strength; framing = degree of control over communication practices, or over selection, organisation, pacing, position, posture, dress, location, and so on). His fascination with this notion of insulation or boundary then produces a long series of tautologies. Here there is space to give only a few typical examples. In each case the connecting or causal words ('then', 'so', 'create', 'regulate', for example) can be replaced by 'is', for Bernstein is merely restating an original definition. I have italicised that part of each sentence which, far from indicating a causal relation, is merely a repetition of the first half of the sentence.

The stronger the insulation between categories, *then the stronger the boundary between one category and another* (p. 313).

Any change in the principle of classification *will require a change in the degree of insulation* (p. 314). (Translation: a change in boundary relations produces a change in boundary relations.)

Changes or variation in framing *produce variations* or *changes in pedagogic practices* (p. 325). (Comment: Of course! *That's* how framing was defined in the first place!)

3 Concepts become reified and causal

Having based his notion of codes on classification and framing, Bernstein quickly turns them into concrete, causal factors which regulate and create human action. His concepts take on a life of their own, determining events (I have noted his remarkably active language on page 121). This slide from speculation into claimed actuality is compounded with the tautological nature of his scheme to produce spurious causal statements. In almost every case, where Bernstein uses active, causal words like 'creates', it is the signal that a tautology is about to be asserted as a causal relation. I have italicised the active verb on which the sentence hinges. The second half of the sentence is merely a restatement of the first half.

Strong frames *reduce* the power of the pupil over what, when and how he receives knowledge, and *increases* the teacher's power in the pedagogical relationships (1971, p. 90). (Translation: tight control by teachers is tight control by teachers.)

Where there is strong classification between education and production, this *creates* the condition for the relative autonomy of education (1977, p. 175).

The degree of insulation is a *crucial regulator* of the relations between categories (1982, pp. 313–4). (Translation: relations between categories regulate relations between categories.)

Bernstein thus creates a concept (or, more precisely, a label), and gives to that concept or label causal powers. In fact, the concept/ label is simply a redefining, re-naming device:

In the same way as relations between categories can be governed by strong or weak classification, so principles of communication can be governed by strong or weak framing (1982, p. 325).

Here is tautology, causality and reification rolled into one. 'Can be governed by' must be replaced by 'are', for 'relations between categories', or 'principles of communication' are Bernstein's *definitions* of classification and framing. The label has intervened and become an explainer in its own right.

4   *Spurious precision*

The claim to rigour and to scientific status is made in two ways. First the highly deterministic nature of Bernstein's language which claims to identify causal links as his concepts variously 'regulate', 'necessarily entail', 'generate', 'transform', 'reproduce', 'select', 'integrate', 'establish', 'change', 'create', 'depends entirely', 'govern', and so on. These confident claims are echoed in his diagrams (see his 1982 paper). The second feature of Bernstein's 'precision' is his production of dubious formulae (noted above and elsewhere in his 1982 paper).[19]

5   *Contradictoriness*

For all its claim to precision, Bernstein's writing suffers from major confusions and contradictions which render it not simply vague, but ungraspable. In blatant reversals he flatly contradicts his own theories, standing them on their head. In his language work the well-known contradiction is:

The ability to switch codes controls the ability to switch roles (p. 129).

versus

. . . if you cannot manage the role, you can't produce the appropriate speech (p. 177).

This is not development of a theory, it is denial. Similarly, in 1982, because of his redefining of classification and insulation the reader is faced with bewildering choice as to which causes which (in fact, because of Bernstein's predilection for tautology, they are the same):

. . . the principle(s) of classification created by the insulation (p. 317).

versus

. . . insulations created by the classification principle (p. 320).

6 Codes are principles

Bernstein's error in advancing his theory of codes is to assume that codes are fundamentally different from 'principles'. For him, codes lie behind any principles or rules of behaviour. Thus he argues that codes:

> generate principles for *distinguishing* between contexts and principles for the *creation and production* of the specialised relationships within a context (1982, p. 306, original italics).

Here, the codes generate principles, lying behind them, giving rise to them. The 'principles' are merely 'recognition rules', or 'realisation rules', or 'ground performance' rules. But Bernstein's codes are mental states and the distinction between codes and principles is false; codes *are* principles. Bernstein simply substitutes 'generates' for 'are', inserting his codes at a level *above* the principles, rules, conceptual schemes, orientations to meaning, which produce language or action. This is erroneous, for codes *are* the principles or rules, syntax or grammar or 'modalities', which govern and maintain action and communication. In short, *codes* are fictitious, interventional, distorting, insertions into explanation. The structuralist enterprise here sadly misleads.

7 The diminution of the individual

We have seen that like all structuralists, Bernstein 'decentres the subject'. For all his denial of the inexorability of inner laws, his pursuit of codes makes people mere tools or puppets in the hands of absent structures which create and govern them:

> Class codes . . . by which and through which subjects are selectively created, positioned and oppositioned (1982, p. 336).

Curiously, Bernstein's own competence and imagination as evidenced in his writings and his influence on educational thought provides clear evidence of the versatility and capability of individuals that his stress on structures and codes denies. Any explanatory scheme which loses sight of human competence and creativity (and capacity for resistance and stubbornness) loses its power. For all his claim to establish the dialectic of the subject and the social, Bernstein's model is highly deterministic, rigid and inhuman. His European structuralism is intellectually exciting and challenging, but its overexpanded concept of *code* and its stress on system at the expense of individual show the limitations of structuralist analyses of education.

Structuralism and teachers

I have been critical of Professor Bernstein and other structuralist theorists. In such criticism I do not intend wholesale dismissal of structuralism, for I am confident it can make important contributions to education. The unfamiliar concepts and high level of abstraction present many difficulties for teachers, so in this section I briefly, and, I hope, simply, set out some ways in which structuralism can aid teachers to understand, evaluate and thus change their practice. In doing so I am only too aware of the dangers of rendering banal and unsubtle what are in fact very complex notions. I therefore hope that, as I make my claims for structuralism in a direct, unargued way, the reader will interpret the assertions in the total context of this book.

Education is centrally concerned to develop understanding and to foster desired attitudes, beliefs and behaviours. *Schooling* represents a socially organised, systematic attempt to educate. It can therefore be analysed from four structural perspectives: structures of thought, structures of feeling, structures of social organisation and structures of human competence (that is to say, concerned respectively with understanding; attitudes, beliefs and values; social structures; and individual capabilities). This is my method of structural analysis (see Chapter 8). To use it in order to understand and evaluate schooling, teachers need to be clear about the *level* and *method* and certain key *concepts*.

1   Level

In identifying structures, be clear about the educational *level* on which you focus. To think of the following levels will help analysis:

(a)   Classroom (e.g. reception infants class, 4T Maths set, tutor group, etc.)
(b)   Department/Faculty (e.g. English Department, Science Faculty)
(c)   School (e.g. Beachside Comprehensive, Mapledene Infants)
(d)   Region (e.g. Blankshire Local Education Authority (LEA), etc.)
(e)   National (e.g. Department of Education and Science (DES), Her Majesty's Inspectorate (HMI), National Union of Teachers (NUT), etc.)

It is possible to carry out structural analysis at any *one* level, although as analyses become more sophisticated they will acknowledge the interrelationships of all (see Lawton, 1979, p. 19).

2 *Method*

At each level seek the structures which underpin action and are evidenced in it. To do this, study a particular 'event' (for example, part of a lesson, a Faculty meeting, a school brochure, Local Education Authority or Department of Education and Science documents). Identify those structures which are evidenced in the event and which are drawn upon and reproduced by participants. The analysis is conducted by considering elements of the four structures of competence, thought, social organisation and feeling. By very close attention to particular events, and by drawing upon experience and already available knowledge, teachers can gain a clearer understanding of the structures within which their practice is set and thus be better able to improve that practice. The characteristics of my method of structural analysis are given in Chapter 8.

3 *Some important concepts*

In spite of the formidable, daunting vocabulary of structuralism, I believe that structural analysis can be carried out by all teachers with little recourse to technical language. However, certain concepts are central and a few of these key assumptions are now briefly re-stated.

Wholes This apparently simple concept can be grossly misleading. It is wise to assume that there are very few homogeneous and consistent structures or wholes. Neither 'the class', nor 'the school', nor 'the Local Education Authority' are unified wholes. Neither too are 'the whole curriculum', nor 'Elizabethan history' nor 'biology', nor 'Infant Schools'. Each is a complex structure containing within itself structures of competence, thought, social organisation and feeling which, *in each specific case*, require analysis. Only 'number', or 'mathematics', or 'chess' and similar systems represent consistent wholes. But in spite of this difficulty it is necessary that all 'events' should be seen in relation to the 'wholes' which contain them and through which we understand them. Mary's actions, whether truanting or dissecting a frog, can only be grasped (and assessed or remedied) through the complex wholes (such as school, discipline, biology) which give meaning to those actions. Teachers need as clear a conception as possible of those structural wholes which enable them to interpret and evaluate both outcomes (for example, an essay) and processes (for example, teacher talk), but must remember that such structures will often be heterogeneous, complex, shifting and even contradictory.

Presence/Absence The notion of presence/absence reminds us that events which are vividly present to us (Mary hitting John, Mary reading the words on the page, the assembled pupils singing a hymn) are produced by, and interpreted through, absent structures. Behind the actions or events we see and experience lie unseen and *unseeable* structures, representing complex cultural wholes which must be grasped and described by intellectual and imaginative reconstructions. Behind the words on the page is the absent language (Saussure's *langue* – see Chapter 2, pages 15–18); behind Mary's action are absent structures of thought, feeling and social relations. But it is important to grasp that both 'absence' and 'behind' are potentially misleading images, for the structures we seek are evidenced *within* each unique event and their existence depends on human action (Althusser's notion of structural causality, pages 55–6, and Chapter 8, pages 138–42). Piaget's identification, through study of children's actions, of the stages of cognitive growth, represents the relations of presence and absence of structures of thought. The four-year-old, comparing different length strips of plasticine and saying 'They're the same', is very obviously *present* to us; but the *absence* that is pre-conceptual thought produces the remark.

Embeddedness Structuralism stresses that individuals are embedded in structures and culture. A useful, but in some ways misleading, analogy is that of language: a word has meaning only in relation to other words, to the whole that is language. Meaning depends on context. So, too, individuals' significance and meaning (for themselves and others) arise from their relations to others and to the structures which contain them. Mary, in the classroom, is both treated, and to be understood, through structures in which she is embedded and which find their expression in her. What are those structures? To hint at only a few: *girl, pupil, sixteen-year-old, Catholic, middle-class, English*; she is in a *comprehensive school*, working in a *maths* set at *algebra*. The structures of thought, feeling and social organisation underpinning and represented in those categories define and shape her. They also *enable* her, for they are the structures through which her own unique characteristics and competences are expressed and given range. She is embedded in those structures but she draws on them and realises them in her own way. To view her thus is to avoid the potential dehumanisation of structuralism, and to remind teachers of the mutual dependence of individual and structure. Mary is embedded in her sex role(s), pupil role(s) and so on, but her own competences enable her (to change the metaphor) to 'play her own variations on the provided theme(s)'.

Transformation Teachers are crucially involved in a process of change. Cognitively, linguistically, emotionally, aesthetically, and socially, schooling as a system is consciously committed to the transformation of the individual pupil: daily, weekly, yearly. Such transformations, structuralism insists, are inevitable consequences of the social and biological system, but schooling attempts to direct, modify and accelerate certain desired transformations and to inhibit others. Transformation, therefore, must be always in teachers' minds; an awareness of what they and their pupils might become, within and through the structures which contain them: thought, feeling and social organisation. Thus the task of structural analysis is to identify the dynamics of change, whether it is at the level of an individual pupil's greater grasp of (say) a mathematical or historical concept (or in her 'better behaviour'), or at the level of change in the whole curriculum of an individual school, or at the level of change in the structure of schooling in a Local Education Authority or a country. By more clearly understanding the structural roots of transformation teachers can predict the direction of change and can adjust their behaviour to attempt to ensure desired outcomes and processes.

Relationships This is at once one of the most popular words in a teacher's vocabulary ('the importance of good relationships') and at the same time one of the most difficult concepts to grasp. After all, it is easy to see concrete objects like things or people, much harder to identify those invisible factors which link them. Structuralism however insists upon relationships rather than things as it seeks the unseen structures of thought, feeling and social organisation which comprise the connective tissue, resource and energy which fuel and enable individual action. Mary and John, struggling with mathematics or reading, are very obviously *present* to the teacher, but they and their activity are understood through webs of relationships, which give meaning to individuals or numbers or words. To re-think classrooms and schools as structures of relationships is not an easy matter, but it provides fresh perspectives which can fruitfully transform practice.

Signs Structuralism gave rise to semiology, the study of signs. Schooling can be regarded as a system of signs. Dress, language, gesture, tests, modes of address, rewards, punishments, time-tables, school subjects, rules, conventions, prospectuses, use of space, furniture, wall displays . . . all *signify*; and the structuralist endeavour becomes one of interpreting these significations.[20] In this respect it corresponds closely to pupil perceptions, for pupils are often sensitively alert to the significance of taken-for-granted practices. ('It ain't as if they don't know your name 'cos you've been there long enough' as the teenager at the beginning of Chapter 5 bitterly complains.) But further, semiology has great relevance for curriculum practice. In the study of all forms of communication – whether film, television, advertising or the words and pictures in school textbooks – the interpretation and analysis of the signs employed by, and embodied in, those media is central.

NOTES

1   Halsey's work on Educational Priority Areas is contained in Department of Education and Science (1972–5). His research into social mobility is in Halsey, Heath and Ridge (1980).
2   Bowles and Gintis (1976).
3   Harris (1979, pp. 163–4).
4   Harris (1979, p. 144).
5   Dale (1976).
6   King (1978).
7   Willis (1977, p. 127).
8   Sharp and Green (1975).
9   Tomlinson (1981); Ford, Mongon and Whelan (1982). The history of special education bears stark witness to the social construction of categories of educational handicap (Tomlinson, 1982; Ford *et al.*, 1982). Most recently, following the recommendation of the War-nock Report (Department of Education and Science, 1978), the 1981 Education Act has abolished all previous categories such as ESN(M) or ESN(S) (Educationally Subnormal, moderate (or mild) or severe) and replaced them with the single classification 'children with learning difficulties'. Warnock's recommendation, and the subsequent legislation, are unlikely to reduce the force of the argument developed on pages 112–15.
10   Squibb (1981).
11   Barton and Tomlinson (1981, p. 208).
12   Barton and Tomlinson (1981, p. 209).

13   Barton and Tomlinson (1981, p. 169).
14   Ford *et al.* (1982, p. 160).
15   Ford *et al.* (1982, p. 125).
16   Ford *et al.* (1982, pp. 127–8).
17   All page references refer to either the 1974 or 1977 collected volumes of Bernstein's writing or to his 1982 paper.

    1974   *Class, Codes and Control. Volume I Theoretical Studies Towards a Sociology of Language* (2nd edition)

    1977   *Class, Codes and Control. Volume III Towards a Theory of Educational Transmission* (2nd edition)
(It is significant that Part II of this volume is entitled: 'Changes in the coding of educational transmissions'.)

    1982   'Codes, modalities and the process of cultural reproduction: a model', in APPLE, MICHAEL W. (ed.) *Cultural and Economic Reproduction in Education: Essays on Class, Ideology and the State* (pp. 304–55).

18   The influence of Mary Douglas on Bernstein cannot be understated. He acknowledges the great importance of her thought in shaping his own, and his binary concepts echo hers (e.g. group/grid). It is interesting that in his 1982 paper he appears to have appropriated and modified her concept of 'voice'. See Douglas (1982).

19   Bernstein's claim to precision is implied in his frequent use of italics. Occasionally this predilection becomes ludicrous. What are we to make of the italicised 'and' in his report that his Research Unit's sample consisted of sixty children 'aged eight *and* eleven' (p. 308). Doubts about spurious precision increase when the original research paper reveals the sample to be fifty-eight children all aged eight (Holland, 1981).

20   Five books which adopt a semiological approach (and which suggest imaginatively how interpretation of signs might be applied to schooling) are Lurie (1982); Martin (1981); Culler (1981); Fiske (1982); Hartley (1982).

8 Structural Analysis

In this chapter I propose structural analysis as a method of studying educational practice with a view to explanation, evaluation and change. In developing the method I have used certain structuralist concepts and assumptions whilst seeking to remedy structuralism's defects. In particular I am concerned to restore the notion of human *competence* to the centre of understanding, and to establish the essential *reciprocity* of individual and society, event and structure. The two concepts of *competence* and *reciprocity* are utterly central in providing valid and realistic accounts of school or social life.

Structural analysis is based on the assumption that any example of human interaction (an *event*) can be analysed to reveal the structures within which individuals live, upon which they draw, through which they exercise their personal competences in their own unique ways, and which they reproduce, recreate, modify and transform. It identifies structures and the dynamic of their relationships with each other and with individuals. Such relationships are complex and subject to great variation. Although patterns are discernible, and although coherent and convincing explanations can be offered for human conduct, such explanations can never reach the levels of precision, completeness and predictability that characterises theories in the natural and physical sciences. Indeed, as we shall see, the stance of structural analysis to the possibility of 'theory' in human affairs is one of scepticism, and its very form (heterogeneous, qualified, offering only partial explanation) echoes the qualities it finds in social phenomena.

Structural analysis is thus a less confident method than traditional social science or even that method proposed by W. G. Runciman (1983) which, in its four-fold approach to understanding (reportage, explanation, description, evaluation), attempts to bridge the gap between those who argue human affairs can be treated methodologically exactly as the natural world and those

who totally reject such an assumption. Whilst agreeing with
Runciman's general position I am less sanguine than he about the
possibility of consensus on what is actually going on, and why, in
society, schools or classrooms.

Structural analysis is then a modest and limited enterprise
concerned with four elements: structures of competence, structures of social organisation, structures of thought and structures of
feeling. Through these four hugely heterogenous structures, social and individual action is realised, constrained and enabled,
evidenced and reproduced. The method identifies, through the
consideration of actual behaviour, those structures which find
unique expression as the source and form of individual action, and
which themselves are revivified and modified by that action. Such
structures do not deny human competence, but include and
acknowledge it. Every event is set within structures, and events
take their form from those structures and can be understood in
terms of them. In contrast to much structuralist method, the
analysis is cultural and historical,[1] concerned to identify in the
unique interactions of individuals the forms that prefigure, contain and explain apparently idiosyncratic, localised, personal encounters. For example, in looking at teachers and pupils in a
classroom, it asks: 'What sorts of structures of thought and feeling
do these individuals draw upon, and exhibit in speech and action?
What social structures constrain and enable their behaviour? How
do *these* individuals give unique expression, through their own
personal characteristics and understandings, to such structures in
pursuit of their own valued goals?' The answers to such questions

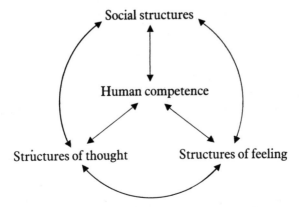

Figure 2 The method of structural analysis

provide material necessary for the evaluation and change of practice. The structures identified themselves prompt questions of worthwhileness and improvement.

The problem with using a word like 'structure' is its suggestion of inflexibility. To assert that there are structures which underpin and influence human behaviour is to be in danger of reducing such behaviour to something puppet-like where man merely responds to impersonal, non-human forces, dancing to structuralist tunes. The word 'structure' conjures up such images and, as we have repeatedly seen, structuralism, in its decentring of the subject, is based on such a view. Structural analysis resists such diminution of the individual, insisting on the flexibility of structures which are seen as human constructions always in dialectical relation, existing independently neither of each other nor of man and woman. Their relationships are complex and interactive, allowing of no simple or single interpretation or prediction, for they correspond to, and embody, that complexity which is life itself. Structural analysis is thus based on distrust of monolithic, all-encompassing, reductive theories, for it assumes that the relationship between person and structure is one of reciprocity, as each individual, in all his/her actions, at once draws upon, embodies, maintains, reproduces and eventually transforms those structures which find their expression in his/her unique behaviour. Such competence and reciprocity show the relation of individual and structure to be one in which the terms and force of the relationship need to be accounted for afresh in each particular instance. To do so requires examination of the problems of agency and reference.

Agency is concerned with what *causes* action, with *why* things happen. Reference concerns the problems of validation: how do we know that an account of an action, an individual, an event, a structure, is a true account? How accurately does it represent reality? Structural analysis approaches agency through the notions of reciprocity and competence. Its partial resolution of reference is through abandoning claim to scientific status and by rejecting pretentions to neat, all-encompassing, non-contradictory theory and all-inclusive categories. Let us examine each in turn.

Agency

Answers to any 'why' question about human affairs are rarely simple, never final. Why does a teacher behave as she does? Why do riots occur on the streets of Brixton and Toxteth? To pose such questions is at once to realise there is no single explanation, no exhaustive account asserting direct cause–effect relationships. Structural analysis offers no such simplicities but claims that two connected assumptions underpin all social explanations: reciprocity and competence. These two assumptions constitute a corrective to structuralism as they re-centre the individual, restoring the notion of capable, knowledgeable actors.

The reciprocity which structural analysis seeks to establish as central to social understanding is implied in Giddens' concept of duality of structure: which relates to:

> . . . the fundamentally recursive character of social life, and expresses the mutual dependence of structure and agency . . . the structural properties of social systems are both the medium and the outcome of the practices that constitute those systems.[2]

Our examination in Chapter 2 of Saussure's concepts of *langue* and *parole* provides an analogy for group and individual, structure and event, and illustrates the notion of reciprocity. *Parole* (speech) represents the unique event, *langue* (language) the corpus of rules and structures underlying it, evidenced in it, enabling it to happen. But in structural analysis the relationship of *langue* and *parole* is not conceived as causal or dependent, as in structural linguistics, but as reciprocal and dialectical. Thus whilst *langue* does produce *parole*, so too it itself is produced and reproduced, maintained and modified by the events which constitute *parole*. The seeming dualities of speech and language, individual and group, event and structure are inextricably, dialectically, related; the exchange is two-way, the connection one of mutual interdependence. And the vital element which makes such interdependence possible is that of human competence.

Structural analysis therefore views the individual as active, creative and self-aware, making and transforming his world. It 'recentres the subject', bringing the individual back to centre stage through the acknowledgment of competence. Unlike structuralism, it incorporates a concept of an active, self-aware, *determining* human being, acting in the web of relationships that is family, school, work, social class, society. Each person is a unique individual, embedded in multi-structured 'wholes' comprising culture, institutions and language. An individual in every action draws upon and realises that culture and, in the act of realisation, renews it, adapts it, recreates it, and eventually transforms it.

Such acknowledgment does not mean that explanations in terms of individuals become paramount. Rather, by recognising competence it resists the dominant trend of structuralism to reduce the individual to a mere puppet, a 'bearer', a unit in a system, a 'cultural dope'. Men, women and children are purposeful, meaning-seeking, reflexive beings who understand the world around them, find sense in it, and indeed *put* sense into it. Their degree of control over their lives is limited, often severely, and structural analysis identifies what constrains them, but it shows also how they actively move within those constraints seeking a realisation of their particular purposes.

To take competence and reciprocity as key concepts in the understanding of human action is to re-cast the structuralist concepts of wholeness, relationships, self-regulation, synchrony and transformation. *Wholes* become heterogeneous, contradictory, elusive, constituted in and by individual action; *relationships* are reconceptualised to take account of the stubborn, resisting competence of purposeful individuals; *self-regulation* becomes not a matter of structuralist laws of a system but of unique human beings realising their own realities in a multiplicity of social contexts; *synchrony* (snapshot) yields to fuller acknowledgment of the dialectical relation of past and present; and *transformations* are seen as effected through the actions of men and women. It is by incorporating the related concepts of reciprocity and human competence into an explanatory scheme that the many problems of agency (social causation) may be approached. Such assumptions will not result in simple cause–effect explanations: social understanding, like the social phenomena it attempts to grasp, is not of such order.

It is now possible to see more clearly why the notion of structure should not be understood as simply constraining. The unfortunate inflexibility about the term we have already noted belies the fluidity, provisionality and resourcefulness that are intended in the use of the term in structural analysis. Structures are to be thought of as complex rule and relational systems which influence, shape and constrain human thought and action, but which simultaneously are the means by which human competence is exercised, by which individual initiative is fostered and facilitated. This concept of competence which articulates structure and event, *langue* and *parole*, individual and collective, restores human consciousness and purposefulness to social explanation, redressing the imbalance of structuralism with its stress on system at the expense of the individual.

Reciprocity and competence afford greater insight into the complexities of educational practice as they resist neat, unitary theorising, and acknowledge teachers and pupils as capable, knowledgeable individuals. Similarly, their embodiment into structural analysis is an antidote to those methods which imply individuals create their own realities virtually single-handed. Whereas structuralism places too much weight on explanatory factors lying outside individuals, much current educational employment of phenomenological approaches overemphasises the individual, neglecting those crucial structural contexts which bear on and constrain individuals. Only if individuals and structures are accorded a necessary reciprocity will our understanding of schooling or society deepen. To lose sight of the individual *or* the structural context of his being is to lose sight of the fact that any explanation of education or society must move in a dynamic that includes person and institution, event and structure, past and present.

If structural analysis places human competence as a central necessary structure of understanding, the limitations of such competence must be acknowledged. At least four may be discerned. First, the ability of any actor to explain the reason for his actions are limited: knowing 'the rules' and being able to act effectively is a quite different operation from being able to render an account of such rules or structures. We all know far more than we can say. Second, an individual's knowledge is limited, particularly with regard to distant events: each person has most knowledge of events closest to home, to his own daily experience. Pupils know little or nothing of Local Education Authorities, or the Department of Education and Science, but the decisions of these institutions affect their lives; and the socio-economic structure weighs heavily on all. Third, actions can have unintended consequences. No pupil (or teacher) goes to school intending to become unhappy; few intend to fail; many do. Fourth, there are what Giddens calls 'unconscious (or unacknowledged) conditions of action' which bear on the individual, and of these ideology and material conditions are particularly powerful. Our ability to act, or to render objective accounts, is necessarily restricted by the limitations imposed by our upbringing, beliefs, culture and social position. Teachers and pupils take for granted the 'rightness' of their own perspectives – even though these often clash. It is this recognition of 'unconscious' motives deriving from structural or psychological forces, of the necessary limitations on human competence, and of intended outcomes, that gives us the clue as to how the problem of reference may be addressed. To this we now turn.

Reference

How do we know that a description of a classroom, or an explanation of the nature and causes of working-class underachievement are true? How do we know that the language we use in such descriptions accurately catches the realities it claims to identify? The response of structural analysis to these problems of *reference* is, for the dogmatist or the seeker after certainty, a disappointing one. It makes only modest claims as to the exhaustiveness of its accounts, freely admitting its own limitations and acknowledging the many difficulties of valid representation. Structural analysis is based on a number of assumptions: that no explanation or description can be exhaustive; that events have multiple causes; that it must reject any claim to be a science; that the relation of language and reality is deeply problematic, and that reality is not constituted simply by language; that contradiction, paradox and fracture are endemic in social life; that literature offers helpful modes of conceiving and depicting reality; and that 'theory' is less helpful than 'principles'.

Partial Explanation and Multiple Causality

There is no limit to the descriptions or explanations that might be offered of a particular event. The validity, usefulness and significance of different accounts will depend on the interests and cultural setting of the describers and explainers. To say this is not to open the floodgates of relativism; rather, it is to acknowledge the diversity of human capacity and activity. The physicist or historian, Marxist or liberal, Christian or Muslim, teacher or pupil, view the same classroom but produce different descriptions and explanations of it. The 'satisfactoriness' of such explanations is much dependent on the interests (in all senses of that term) of the audience. Again, this is not to reduce truth to mere consensus; the physicist's explanation is true whether the hearers are interested or not. What I am saying is that *truths*, rather than *the* truth, characterises social life; and different truths will have greater significance and appeal for some listeners than for others.

Further, no explanation is ever complete, even though common-sense, taken-for-granted assumptions, time and habit ensure that in practice we nearly always act as if it were. We are simply not interested in producing or hearing the infinite number of explanations possible for any single event. It would be too boring. But we should not lose sight of the fact that the brief explanations we prefer, the labels 'trivial', 'irrelevant' we apply to other explanations, rest on a web of taken-for-granted, culturally conditioned assumptions. Thus when we undertake structural analysis of a classroom event, the truths and significances revealed are not eternal, but tied to the interests and preoccupations of twentieth-century Western culture.

Structural analysis finds Althusser's notion of *overdetermination* (see Chapter 4, pages 54–5) helpful, as it suggests the many causes which contribute to (overdetermine) a particular event. The narrative for any event is woven of many strands. Structural analysis rejects any notion of single cause in social explanation; account must be taken of material, ideological and cultural factors. When a teacher sets a mathematical problem for a pupil, or when he disciplines the pupil, the explanations (reasons, causes) for his actions are multiple, and the stories that *could* be told which lead up to the event are legion. The ones preferred (or appropriate) will very often depend on the *level* at which such explanations are offered. Very few teachers would be interested in the physical or biological antecedents of action, most are indifferent to sociological explanations concerned with 'distant' social structures. For both teacher and pupil more local, person-based explanations are preferred. Structural analysis offers the opportunity to explore the deep structure of those familiar events.

Structural Analysis is not a Science

Structural analysis does not lay claim to the status of science. It rejects that chimera which has so bedazzled theorists who believe that by describing their concepts, methods, findings as 'scientific', the validity of their descriptions and explanations will be enhanced. Structuralists, Marxists and social scientists have long been bewitched by such fantasy. They have seen the success and prestige of the natural sciences and have mistakenly sought to emulate them. Structural analysis is not *anti*-science, but is sensitive to the immense variety of activities labelled 'scientific', and therefore adopts a more modest stance echoing the provisionality and fluidity of science stressed by such different writers as Popper and Kuhn.[3]

Structural analysis is not a rejection of the empirical method, because it accepts the necessity for careful observation and such measurement as is possible, but its stance to 'testing', to the claims of scientific precisions in social matters, is one of scepticism. For the majority of educational research (and for all *teacher-conducted* research) aping of scientific procedures has been a misguided, distorting and time-wasting enterprise. Empiricism *is* indispensable, but its limitations and its demands should be acknolwedged. All too often in teacher-conducted research such acknowledgment is not made.

Scientific educational research often seeks to 'correct' everyday, common-sense views of classrooms. This is not the stance of structural analysis which seeks rather to enlarge such views, and to respect the authenticity of everyday language and participants' understandings. To reject the label of science is to acknowledge the reduced predictive ability of structural analysis. Such consequence is accepted with equanimity; the possibility of prediction of human affairs comparable with prediction in the natural or physical sciences is unrealistic. The recognition of human competence as a major element in social life itself acts to reduce the possibility of prediction. Education is a cultural phenomenon, and cultural analysis requires methods, interpretations and judgments which are only very partially available or enabled through the approaches of science.

Language and Reality

For all its acknowledgment of its own limitations, structural analysis does assume that through language the world can be described, actions appropriately identified, events truthfully depicted. Valid accounts can be offered even if the truths identified are always partial, always humanly constructed. But while experience can be rendered through language, language does not itself alone comprise the world. In this acknowledgment of action, of a world other than that rendered through language, structural analysis identifies, but does not resolve, the problem of the relationship of language and experience. It is neither a simple matter of correspondence nor coherence. Whilst intimately related, the relationship of 'words and things' is infinitely complex and that complexity is acknowledged by contrasting structural analysis with structuralism. Unlike structuralism, the method of structural analysis assumes 'a world elsewhere'. In contrast, structuralism's lack of a theory of reference is notorious. Its insistence on a closed world, a system of language and ideas, evacuates meaning, as explanation is pursued in terms *solely* of the containing system. Structuralism's concern for internal coherence can reject the possibility of external reference. In literature for example, as we saw in Chapter 6, structures of language take precedence over meaning. Such restriction is inadequate for literature and is even more unsatisfactory for education. Schools are not closed worlds. Any extended understanding must have reference to those outside interconnecting worlds of home, work, culture, ideology, economics. Such worlds are not reducible merely to their language systems, for language only partly comprises each. The paradox is that language is overwhelmingly our dominant mode of reference to those (partially language constituted) worlds. Structural analysis acknowledges reference (i.e. connects language and reality) in its stress on the competent human actor, and its structures of social organisation, thought and feeling. In so doing it both rejects a monolithic emphasis on system and recognises that language is not a transparent, innocent medium of depiction. To use a striking image from Brian Friel's *Translations*,[4] structural analysis attempts to ensure that its linguistic contour matches the landscape of fact. But its mapping of fact is undertaken with awareness of the complex reciprocity of language and experience. Language helps to create the realities it describes, especially in schooling!

Fracture, Paradox, Contradiction

The descriptions given or meanings disclosed by structural analysis are not unproblematic unities or coherences, but are often characterised by contradiction, ambiguity and paradox. Structural analysis embraces what structuralism and other unitary theories dismiss as 'fragmentation'. In such schemes fragmentation implies randomness, non-meaningfulness: it is used as a pejorative term by those who espouse 'wholeness' and see any departure from such indivisibility as aberrant. In contrast, structural analysis' pluralism asserts that the incompatibilities of differing groups, ideologies, beliefs, structures, cultures, bear witness to the plenitude of human action and human understanding. Classrooms reflect that plenitude, and structural analysis seeks to identify its paradoxes and fractures, disjunctions and uncertainties. The consequence of placing the meaning-seeking, meaning-endowing individual, with his full array of competences, at the centre of explanation is to accept fragmentation, for it is in competence itself that the fractures and contradictions of social life have their origin and find expression. The paradoxes of schooling are a testament to human competence, for competence disputes single, simple answers to the question: 'How should children be educated?' Each person who undertakes structural analysis will have his own preferences: what the method does is to enable him to examine the roots of those preferences, and identify the structural conditions of current practice and future change. Such analysis may reveal that any individual's command over structures is limited in the extreme. As we are 'born into language' so too are we born into structures of thought, feeling and social organisation. However, the centrality accorded to human competence is some guarantee of the possibility for the individual to gain greater control over his life. That possibility may be severely bounded by interests, power and sheer contingency, but structural analysis is a first necessary step to provide the understanding which precedes change.

Literature and Reality

Structural analysis draws upon certain assumptions and methods of literature and literary criticism to illuminate its portrayals and explanations. To say this is not to argue that structural analysis draws exclusively on, or attempts to emulate, the assumptions and methods of artistic expression. To do so would be to reproduce the errors of that practice known as 'curriculum criticism'.[5] Rather, it is guided by several characteristics of literature and criticism.

It takes from literary criticism the practice of close, detailed scrutiny of the text. If we substitute for 'text', the 'event', or 'classroom', the potential illumination that literary structuralism *can* provide is evident. Its irreverence, or preference for analysis over celebration, is concerned to show what is there, rather than what we wish to be. The identification of the conventions of literature, shows that much explanation can be done in terms of those internal rules. The analogy is fruitful, for much of teachers' and pupils' behaviour can be understood, indeed must be understood, *because* they are teachers and pupils. The meaning of their actions is given by the context.

The comparable method is that of *practical criticism* of poetry or prose. In structural analysis this becomes a very detailed consideration of a small piece of social experience which reveals the deep structures that influence, shape and are themselves influenced by the event. Such close scrutiny respects the characteristic element of literature: its particularity, its concern with unique individuals, uniquely engaged. Structural analysis is a similar refusal to allow the particular (the actual behaviour of individuals) to be obscured by the general and the abstract. We cannot explain Mary Jones' actions unless Mary Jones herself is central to the explanation. But its endeavour, unlike literature (but like some types of literary criticism), is overtly to link the particular with the general. As Goldmann and Williams have convincingly shown, in the particularities of literature can be glimpsed the correspondence (or *homologies*) with cultural form.[6]

Structural analysis, like literature, draws upon two crucial elements of understanding which are fundamentally elusive: event and structure (or moment and totality). Events or moments vanish at the instant they appear, disappearing into history that can only be recalled in some mode other than the event itself. Classrooms change, second to second, recoverable only in different forms as words or pictures. Totality or structure are elusive wholes that can never be fully charted or grasped. The 'wholes' that are 'language' or 'education' are never fully present. This elusiveness is one of the puzzling paradoxes of social understanding that must be understood and accepted. We know, and yet we do not know. Taken together with the conscious and unconscious awarenesses that make up human competence, it directs us to develop greater caution about attempts to imitate science in our understanding of the individual in society, and to value more John Keats' 'negative capability': 'that is, when a man is capable of being in uncertainties, mysteries, doubts, without any irritable reaching after fact and reason'.[7]

This capacity, which Keats attributed to Shakespeare, implies a tolerance of ambiguity, a capacity to suspend judgment in order to report faithfully an experience, a receptivity and submission which extends awareness and which allows deeper penetration of reality in its acknowledgment of complexity and paradox. Structural analysis claims some very modest achievement of these ideals is possible. To do so implies a critical stance to the notion of theory itself.

Theory or Principles?

'Theory' is knowledge the form of which is elaborated, abstract, systematic, internally coherent, predictive, of universal application, expressed in technical, self-conscious and precise language. I am sceptical of the claims implied in such notions of theory, whether of literature, society, or schooling. Notwithstanding this scepticism, structural analysis identifies patterns, regularities and consistencies, presenting a coherent narrative that links particularity and general. It claims typicality in the consideration of the unique case. The structures it sees as underlying practice (and, reciprocally, being drawn upon, realised and recreated by individuals) have forms less to be expressed as 'theory' than as 'principles'. My preference for principles is that they have more flexibility and allow more for exception and contradiction than does theory. The complexity and variability of practice of schooling should not be underestimated or diminished. Such diminution is all too often the effect of theory and theorising: a striving for intellectual neatness, which, in its passion for tidying-up, for inclusion, trivialises and reduces human activity to a uniformity it does not possess. Structural analysis shows that significant structures do exist but their very nature guarantees both pattern and variation. The looser term 'principles' avoids the restriction and neatness which 'theory' implies.

Structural Analysis and Schooling

I have set out elsewhere (Gibson, 1981b) an example of structural analysis based on original material from a two-year Social Science Research Council research project. I have also given (in Chapters 5 and 7) some indications of ways in which structures can be recovered from existing published research. To illustrate how the method can be used to identify structures in classroom encounters, I reproduce below a brief extract from a very much longer structural analysis based on an infant teacher's own recording of her classroom activity. The full analysis is available in Gibson (1982). It shows how, from a transcript of a twenty-five minute lesson, structures of competence, thought, feeling and social organisation can be seen to constrain and enable pupils and their teacher as they draw upon, express and reproduce those structures in action. Mrs Jones and her four, five and six year olds are talking about water. The extract is from the analysis of *structures of thought*.

The teacher has placed a number of balls of different composition in the water: some float high, others sink almost to the bottom: each ball floats at a different level.

(90)	*Teacher*	Are they all floating the same way?
(91)	*Children*	Yes!
		Yes!! (Chorus)
(92)	*Teacher*	Do you think they are?
(93)	*Children*	No!
		Yes!
		No!
		Yes!
(94)	*Jonathan*	Oh, that ball isn't!
(95)	*Teacher*	Could you tell us why it isn't? Jonathan?
(96)	*Jonathan*	'Cos it's near the edge.
(97)	*Teacher*	Can you say it a bit more clearly why it isn't? Can you put it another way? That one. Is that floating in a different way to the others? . . . if you look carefully at it, there is something a bit special about the way that one is floating. Tracy, can you tell us anything?
(98)	*Tracy*	It's going round.
(99)	*Teacher*	It's going round as well, but I pushed it. Joan?
(100)	*Joan*	It's got some patch, it's got.
(101)	*Teacher*	(No, you sit down.) It's what Joan?
(102)	*Joan*	It moves with the wind.
(103)	*Teacher*	It moves across to the corner in the wind, but look at how much of the ball is in the water. Look at the big ball – (No, I want you to sit down, sit down.)
(104)	*A child*	I moved it!
(105)	*Teacher*	Shh, shh.
(106)	A child	I moved it!
(107)	*Teacher*	Nathaniel is looking from the side. Would you like to come this side, Nathaniel, and then you will see clearer. That's a very good idea.

. . .

(109)	*Teacher*	Why do you think that this ball seems to float much lower in the water than the others that are floating? John?
(110)	*John*	'Cos . . . it's got a weight in it.

The extract shows very clearly the teacher's concern that the pupils should engage a particular mode of thought: scientific, secular, rational. The assumptions of speech are in marked contrast to her attitude to cognitive style at other times of the day, for example when story-telling or commenting on art work, or at prayers.

For a sustained period Mrs Jones subtly rejects children's answers which are irrelevant or inappropriate to this preferred mode of thought. She wants to know why the other balls are not floating in the same way as the one indicated and her judgment of answers will be shaped by the structure of scientific thought. One child (Jonathan) replies:

(96)   'Cos it's near the edge.

The teacher doesn't say he's wrong, but invites him to put it in another way. He has made a correct *observation*, but it is not an appropriate answer to her 'why' question. After a pause Tracy volunteers:

(98)   It's going round.

Again the reply is wrong. The teacher wants not a description of mere external appearances, but some explanation in terms of physical properties (which, later in their school careers the pupils will meet as 'specific density'). As with her reply to Jonathan, she does not tell Tracy directly that she is wrong, but gives an explanation ('I pushed it'). Now Joan offers:

(100)   It's got some patch.

Again, the explanation is scientifically wrong, and the structure of thought within which the teacher is operating makes her convey to Joan that her first attempt is not correct; so Joan tries again:

(102)   It moves with the wind.

Once more, the teacher avoids direct correction. The child's reply is again possibly an accurate observation but not relevant to the question asked. Another child calls out

(104/106)   I moved it!

But once again Mrs Jones, by ignoring this reply, shows it is inappropriate because of the structure of thought she deems appropriate – indeed *is* appropriate.

What we are seeing here is the rejection of ways of thinking: magic, anthropomorphism, human agency, that will be quite acceptable at other times of the school day. Through the children's close observation the teacher wishes them to advance some scientific explanation of what they see, not merely report *what* they see. As a teacher she deems such a way of thinking valuable (and it certainly will be utterly vital to the success of the children's future educational careers that they learn to engage such a structure when appropriate). Thus, the structure of thought itself shapes her actions, prompts her replies. Mrs Jones draws upon it, teaching in her own personal style, but behind that individual style can be clearly seen the thought structure that informs her words and deeds. Nathaniel is rewarded for his close observation

(107)   That's a very good idea.

But it is John who produces an answer nearer what she wants

(110)   'Cos . . . it's got a weight in it.

Although this is not the technically correct answer, it is *some* way towards a notion of density. Put together with 'air' it will give a rough scientific explanation to why some things float and others sink. For children of this age it is probably appropriate. (Presumably, at this age level, an appropriate explanation is in terms of 'the stuff it's made of', 'how that stuff is arranged', and 'how it's placed on the water', very rough indicators of what will later on in school be given much sharper technical definition.) But it is the structure of thought that we should note. Not only is it not 'magic', but it is structured in a particular way: abstract, theoretical, law-like, predictive and applicable to the natural and physical world . . . in other words, scientific. Clearly, the children have grasped the *form* of the teacher's 'Why?' question: they know a 'because' is needed to start their reply: verbal competence is highly developed. What they find difficult is engaging the thought form that will loom so importantly in their future schooling. The teacher seeks an understanding that seems, at this age, to be beyond them (interestingly, a Schools Council/Nuffield Science Booklet specifically suggests that such a 'why' question is inappropriate to put to young children). But the *form* of the required answer is much in the teacher's mind, working powerfully to influence her actions.

The point I am making is that in asking why one thing floats differently from another the teacher is implicitly seeking two things: first, the engagement of a particular *way* of thinking, a structure of thought (the empirical–rational mode of science) to the exclusion of other structures; and second, the expression of that mode in a particular case. She wants the children to move from direct observation to some general conclusion that will have law-like application. Although her own preference for 'weight' and 'air' may be open to criticism and correction (an example of how structural analysis identifies opportunity for improvement), what is important is the structure of thought the teacher is seeking to engage. In these particular interchanges we see the influence of cognitive structures that will take different form when later Mrs Jones talks with her class about ogres or postmen or King Canute or the number seven. (The analysis now proceeds to discuss the structure of thought which informs such utterances as 'Shh, shh', 'sit down', 'Would you like to come this side?', and so on, and to show how, as schooling progresses, it is increasingly formally marked off from other structures, and is given specific content and distinct validation criteria.)

Structural analysis is therefore offered partly as a corrective to one of the besetting errors of teacher-conducted research: the over-collection of data. All too often, teachers who undertake research gather huge quantities of data: test results, interview transcripts, observational schedule results. All too often, they do not know *why* they collect it, or what to do with it. As a result, most of the data collected lies unexamined, unanalysed, representing a waste of both the teacher's and the interviewee's time. In these cases, the action of data collection is a substitute for thought. The time spent collecting is out of all proportion to time given to thinking of purpose or analysis. The method of structural analysis attempts to reverse the balance. It can be employed as a policy of minimum data, in its concern for very careful scrutiny and rigorous thought about particularly focused items or events. In such tight focus, the teacher can draw upon an already rich store of experience (and upon data already publicly available) and can, through the flexibility and openness afforded by the method, undertake his or her own classroom or school action-research in an authentic and legitimate manner.[8]

Conclusion

Notwithstanding all the criticism I have made throughout this book, I am convinced that structuralism offers to teachers (and others) an initially difficult but, once grasped, powerful mode of understanding, evaluating and transforming practice. To be aware of the structures within which teachers and pupils work is to possess some organic measures against which individual performance – whether of child, teacher, department, school – can be evaluated. For example, at the level of classroom teaching Jerome Bruner has powerfully made the case for teachers knowing – and attempting to teach – the fundamental structure of a subject.[9] His reasons are, first, because it makes the subject more comprehensible; second, because it promotes better memorisation and utilisation; third, because it acts as a model for understanding other things; and fourth, because it narrows the gap between elementary and advanced knowledge. Similarly, at the level of the whole school experience of pupils, we can note the practice of 'shared time' at Stantonbury Comprehensive School.[10] Here, in a conscious effort to avoid what the head and staff saw as fragmentation of pupil experience, a holistic approach was adopted to ensure that secondary pupils spent a good deal of their time each week with the same team of teachers. Further, at the levels of both school and society we can note the systematic efforts of writers such as Denis Lawton (1983) to work out a coherent model for the construction of a whole curriculum.

To understand structures is to possess some insight into ways in which change can be made towards preferred processes, performances and outcomes. The degree of precision with which evaluation and prescription take place will vary. At the level of pupil understanding of certain mathematical concepts, the teacher's grasp of the structures of number, space or time will permit (or limit) assessment of pupil performance and enable prescription of courses of action to improve those achievements. When the teacher or head considers the structures of feeling which comprise the ethos of the classroom or the school, or the varied structures which underpin any notion of the whole curriculum, questions of evaluation and change are complex in the extreme. Nonetheless, without conscious awareness and consideration of such structures, the tasks of improving the ethos of the school and the curriculum cannot be adequately undertaken, for it is through understanding these structures that choices can be made more rationally. Structuralism, for all its many faults, provides fresh dimensions to the study and practice of education. My aim in this book has been to show how those new perspectives can be obtained through consideration of the four structures of competence, thought, feeling and social organisation.

NOTES

1 An interesting and, I think, complementary method is that of cultural analysis (Lawton, 1983) which addresses itself very directly to questions of curriculum construction.
2 Giddens (1979, p. 69).
3 Popper (1968); Kuhn (1962).
4 Friel (1981). Brian Friel's play is a fascinating dramatic exploration of the relationships between language and reality as English Army Survey officers prepare a new map replacing Irish with English place-names.
5 Curriculum criticism (an attempt to use aesthetic and literary

approaches to schooling) has resulted in some very weird material: see Gibson (1981a).

6 The correspondence between literature and society is clearly put in Goldmann (1975):

[my hypothesis is] the homology between the structure of the classical novel and the structure of exchange in the liberal economy . . . The novel form seems to me, in effect, to be the transposition on the literary plane of everyday life in the individualistic society created by market production. There is a rigorous homology between the literary form of the novel and the everyday relation between man and commodities in general (pp. 1 and 7).

See also Williams (1961, 1980).

7 John Keats in a letter to his brother, 22 December 1817. See Ward (1963).

8 John Elliott in particular has long been active in encouraging teachers to develop educational theory based on their own practice. Structural analysis offers one method for them so to do. See Elliott (1983).

9 Bruner (1960).

10 See Open University (1982) for the background to Stantonbury. 'The Burston School Strike' in Open University (1976) is an excellent example of a school-based curriculum development project undertaken in Stantonbury's 'shared time'.

Bibliography

ALTHUSSER, L. (1969) *For Marx*. London: Allen Lane.

ALTHUSSER, L. (1972) 'Ideology and Ideological State Apparatuses', in COSIN, B. R. *Education: Structure and Society*. Harmondsworth: Penguin Books (pp. 242–80).

ALTHUSSER, L. and BALIBAR, E. (1970) *Reading Capital*. London: New Left Books.

APPLE, MICHAEL W. (ed.) (1982) *Cultural and Economic Reproduction in Education: Essays on Class, Ideology and the State*. London: Routledge and Kegan Paul.

ATKINSON, PAUL (1981) 'Bernstein's Structuralism'. *Educational Analysis*, 3, 1, pp. 85–95.

BALL, STEPHEN J. (1981) *Beachside Comprehensive: A Case Study of Secondary Schooling*. Cambridge: Cambridge University Press.

BARTON, LEN and TOMLINSON, SALLY (eds) (1981) *Special Education: Policy, Practices and Social Issues*. New York: Harper and Row.

BARTON, LEN and WALKER, STEPHEN (eds) (1981) *Schools, Teachers and Teaching*. London: Falmer Press.

BARTON, LEN and WALKER, STEPHEN (eds) (1983) *Race, Class and Education*. London: Croom Helm.

BARTHES, ROLAND (1967) *Elements of Semiology*. London: Jonathan Cape.

BARTHES, ROLAND (1972a) *Mythologies*. London: Jonathan Cape.

BARTHES, ROLAND (1972b) *Critical Essays*. Evanston, Ill.: Northwestern University Press.

BECKER, HOWARD S. *et al.* (1961) *Boys in White: Student Culture in a Medical School*. Chicago, Ill.: University of Chicago Press.

BELSEY, CATHERINE (1980) *Critical Practice*. London: Methuen.

BERGER, PETER and LUCKMANN, THOMAS (1967) *The Social Construction of Reality*. Harmondsworth: Penguin Books.

BERNSTEIN, BASIL (1974) *Class, Codes and Control. Volume 1: Theoretical Studies towards a Sociology of Language* (2nd edition). London: Routledge and Kegan Paul.

BERNSTEIN, BASIL (1977) *Class, Codes and Control. Volume 3: Towards a Theory of Educational Transmission* (2nd edition). London: Routledge and Kegan Paul.

BERNSTEIN, BASIL (1982) 'Codes, modalities and the process of cultural reproduction: a model', in APPLE, MICHAEL (ed.) *Cultural and Economic Reproduction in Education*. London: Routledge and Kegan Paul (pp. 309–55).

BERNSTEIN, RICHARD J. (1976) *The Restructuring of Social and Political Theory*. Oxford: Basil Blackwell.

BLOOM, HAROLD et al. (1979) *Deconstruction and Criticism*. London: Routledge and Kegan Paul.

BODEN, MARGARET A. (1979) *Piaget*. London: Collins (Fontana).

BOULTON, MARJORIE (1982) *The Anatomy of Poetry* (2nd edition). London: Routledge and Kegan Paul.

BOWLES, S. and GINTIS, H. (1976) *Schooling in Capitalist America*. New York: Basic Books.

BRUNER, JEROME S. (1960) *The Process of Education*. Cambridge, Mass.: Harvard University Press.

CENTRE FOR CONTEMPORARY CULTURAL STUDIES (1982) *The Empire Strikes Back: Race and Racism in 70s Britain*. London: Hutchinson.

CHOMSKY, NOAM (1965) *Aspects of the Theory of Syntax*. Cambridge, Mass.: MIT Press.

CLARKE, SIMON (1981) *The Foundations of Structuralism: A Critique of Levi-Strauss and the Structuralist Movement*. Brighton: Harvester Press.

COWAN, Q. A. (1978) *Piaget with Feeling: Cognitive, Social and Emotional Dimensions*. New York: Holt, Rinehart and Winston.

CULLER, JONATHAN (1975) *Structuralist Poetics: Structuralism, Linguistics and the Study of Literature*. London: Routledge and Kegan Paul.

CULLER, JONATHAN (1976) *Saussure*. London: Collins (Fontana).

CULLER, JONATHAN (1981) *The Pursuit of Signs: Semiotics, Literature, Deconstruction*. London: Routledge and Kegan Paul.

CULLER, JONATHAN (1983) *On Deconstruction: Theory and Criticism after Structuralism*. London: Routledge and Kegan Paul.

DALE, ROGER et al. (1976) *Schooling and Capitalism*. London: Routledge and Kegan Paul.

DEPARTMENT OF EDUCATION AND SCIENCE (1963) *Higher Education* (The Robbins Report). London: Her Majesty's Stationery Office.

DEPARTMENT OF EDUCATION AND SCIENCE (1967) *Children and their Primary Schools* (The Plowden Report). London: Her Majesty's Stationery Office.

DEPARTMENT OF EDUCATION AND SCIENCE (1972–5) *Educational Priority*, Volumes 1–5. London: Her Majesty's Stationery Office.

DEPARTMENT OF EDUCATION AND SCIENCE (1978) *Special Educational Needs* (The Warnock Report). London: Her Majesty's Stationery Office.

DERRIDA, JACQUES (1978) *Writing and Difference*. London: Routledge and Kegan Paul.

DONALDSON, MARGARET (1978) *Children's Minds*. London: Collins (Fontana).

DOUGLAS, MARY (1982) *In the Active Voice*. London: Routledge and Kegan Paul.

EAGLETON, TERRY (1978) *Criticism and Ideology: A Study in Marxist Literary Theory*. London: Verso/New Left Books.

EAGLETON, TERRY (1983) *Literary Theory: An Introduction*. Oxford: Basil Blackwell.

ELLIOTT, JOHN (1983) *Legitimation Crisis and the Growth of Educational Action Research*. Cambridge: Cambridge Institute of Education (mimeograph).

ELLIOTT, JOHN, BRIDGES, DAVID, EBBUTT, DAVID, GIBSON, REX, and NIAS, JENNIFER (1981) *School Accountability*. London: Grant McIntyre.

EVANS, K. M. (1962) *Sociometry and Education*. London: Routledge and Kegan Paul.

FISKE, JOHN (1982) *Introduction to Communication Studies*. London: Methuen.

FORD, JULIENNE, MONGON, DENIS and WHELAN, MAURICE (1982) *Special Education and Social Control: Invisible Disasters*. London: Routledge and Kegan Paul.

FRIEL, BRIAN (1981) *Translations*. London: Faber.

GADAMER, H. G. (1975) *Truth and Method*. London: Sheed and Ward.

GELLNER, ERNEST (1974) *Legitimation of Belief*. Cambridge: Cambridge University Press.

GEUSS, RAYMOND (1981) *The Idea of a Critical Theory*. Cambridge: Cambridge University Press.

GIBSON, REX (1979) 'Review'. *Journal of Further and Higher Education*, 3, 2, pp. 78–85.

GIBSON, REX (1981a) 'Curriculum criticism: misconceived theory, ill-advised practice'. *Cambridge Journal of Education*, 11, 3, pp. 190–210.

GIBSON, REX (1981b) 'Structures of accountability', in ELLIOTT, JOHN *et al. School Accountability*. London: Grant McIntyre.

GIBSON, REX (1982) 'Structural analysis of an infant water play session', in GIBSON, REX *Social Understanding*. Cambridge: Cambridge Institute of Education (pp. 278–306) (mimeograph).

GIDDENS, ANTHONY (1976) *New Rules of Sociological Method*. London: Hutchinson.

GIDDENS, ANTHONY (1977) *Studies in Social and Political Theory*. London: Hutchinson.

GIDDENS, ANTHONY (1979) *Central Problems in Social Theory: Action, Structure and Contradiction in Social Analysis*. London: Macmillan.

GIDDENS, ANTHONY (1981) *A Contemporary Critique of Historical Materialism*. London: Macmillan.

GIDDENS, ANTHONY (1982) 'Power, the dialectic of control and class structuration', in GIDDENS, ANTHONY and MACKENZIE, GAVIN (eds) *Social Class and the Division of Labour*. Cambridge: Cambridge University Press (pp. 29–45).

GIDDENS, ANTHONY (1983) *Profiles and Critiques in Social Theory*. London: Macmillan.

GIDDENS, ANTHONY and MACKENZIE, GAVIN (eds) (1982) *Social Class and the Division of Labour*. Cambridge: Cambridge University Press.

GOLDMANN, LUCIEN (1964) *The Hidden God*. London: Routledge and Kegan Paul.

GOLDMANN, LUCIEN (1975) *Towards a Sociology of the Novel*. London: Tavistock.

GRACE, GERALD (1978) *Teachers, Ideology and Social Control*. London: Routledge and Kegan Paul.

GRANT, DAMIEN (1970) *Realism*. London: Methuen.

GREEN, ANDRE (1979) *The Tragic Effect: The Oedipus Complex in Tragedy*. Cambridge: Cambridge University Press.

GRONLUND, NORMAN E. (1959) *Sociometry in the Classroom*. New York: Harper and Bolton.

HALL, S., HOBSON, D., LOWE, A. and WILLIS, P. (1980) *Culture, Media, Language: Working Papers in Cultural Studies 1972–9*. London: Hutchinson.

HALSEY, A. H., FLOUD, J. and ANDERSON, C. A. (1961) *Education, Economy and Society*. New York: Free Press.

HALSEY, A. H., HEATH, A. F. and RIDGE, S. M. (1980) *Origins and Destinations: Family, Class and Education in Modern Britain*. Oxford: Clarendon Press.

HAMMERSLEY, M. and WOODS, P. (eds) (1976) *The Process of Schooling*. London: Routledge and Kegan Paul.

HARGREAVES, DAVID (1967) *Social Relations in a Secondary School*. London: Routledge and Kegan Paul.

HARGREAVES, DAVID (1982) *The Challenge for the Comprehensive School*. London: Routledge and Kegan Paul.

HARRIS, KEVIN (1979) *Education and Knowledge: The Structured Misrepresentation of Reality*. London: Routledge and Kegan Paul.

HARTLEY, JOHN (1982) *Understanding News*. London: Methuen.

HELD, DAVID.(1982) *Introduction to Critical Theory: Horkheimer to Habermas*. London: Hutchinson.

HIRST, P. H. (1975) *Knowledge and the Curriculum*. London: Routledge and Kegan Paul.

HOLLAND, JANET (1981) 'Social class and changes in orientation to meaning'. *Sociology*, 15, 1, pp. 1–18.

JAKOBSON, ROMAN (1973) 'Two aspects of language: metaphor and metonomy', in GRAS, VERNON W. (ed.) *European Literary Theory and Practice*. New York: Delta (pp. 119–29).

JAKOBSON, ROMAN and JONES, L. (1970) *Shakespeare's Verbal Art in 'Th' Expense of Spirit'*. The Hague, Netherlands: Mouton.

JAY, MARTIN (1973) *The Dialectical Imagination*. London: Heinemann.

JOSIPOVICI, GABRIEL (1979) *The World and the Book: A Study of Modern Fiction* (2nd edition). London: Macmillan.

KARABEL, JEROME and HALSEY, A. H. (1977) *Power and Ideology in Education*. New York: Oxford University Press.

KAROL, K. S. (1980) 'The tragedy of the Althussers'. *New Left Review*, 124, pp. 93–5.

KERMODE, FRANK (1979) *The Genesis of Secrecy: On the Interpretation of Narrative*. Cambridge, Mass.: Harvard University Press.

KETTLE, ARNOLD (1967) *An Introduction to the English Novel* (2nd edition). London: Hutchinson.

KING, RONALD (1978) *All Things Bright and Beautiful? A Sociological Study of Infants' Classrooms*. New York: John Wiley.

KRYLOV, B. (ed.) (1976) *Marx and Engels: On Literature and Art*. Moscow: Progress Publishers.

KUHN, THOMAS S. (1962) *The Structure of Scientific Revolutions*. Chicago, Ill.: University of Chicago Press.

KURZWEIL, EDITH (1980) *The Age of Structuralism: Levi-Strauss to Foucault*. New York: Columbia University Press.

LACAN, JACQUES (1977) *The Four Fundamental Concepts of Psychoanalysis*. London: Hogarth Press.

LAVERS, ANNETTE (1982) *Roland Barthes: Structuralism and After*. London: Methuen.

LAWTON, DENIS (1979) *The End of the Secret Garden? A Study in the Politics of the Curriculum*. London: University of London Institute of Education.

LAWTON, DENIS (1981) *An Introduction to Teaching and Learning*. London: Hodder and Stoughton.

LAWTON, DENIS (1983) *Curriculum Studies and Educational Planning*. London: Hodder and Stoughton.

LEACH, EDMUND (1970) *Levi-Strauss*. London: Collins (Fontana).

LEACH, EDMUND (1973) 'Structuralism in social anthropology', in ROBEY, DAVID (ed.) *Structuralism: An Introduction*. Oxford: Clarendon Press.

LEAVIS, F. R. (1972) *The Great Tradition*. Harmondsworth: Penguin Books.

LEITCH, VINCENT B. (1983) *Deconstructive Criticism: An Advanced Introduction*. London: Hutchinson.

LEVI-STRAUSS, CLAUDE (1963) *Totemism*. Boston, Mass.; Beacon Press.

LEVI-STRAUSS, CLAUDE (1966) *The Savage Mind*, Chicago, Ill.: University of Chicago Press.

LEVI-STRAUSS, CLAUDE (1968) *Structural Anthropology. Volume 1*. London: Allen Lane.

LEVI-STRAUSS, CLAUDE (1969) *Elementary Structures of Kinship*. Boston, Mass.: Beacon Press.

LEVI-STRAUSS, CLAUDE (1970) *Mythology. Volume 1 The Raw and the Cooked*. London: Jonathan Cape.

LEVI-STRAUSS, CLAUDE (1973) *Mythology. Volume 2 From Honey to Ashes*. London: Jonathan Cape.

LEVI-STRAUSS, CLAUDE (1977) *Structural Anthropology. Volume 2.* London: Allen Lane.
LEVI-STRAUSS, CLAUDE (1978) *Mythology. Volume 3 The Origins of Table Manners.* London: Jonathan Cape.
LEVI-STRAUSS, CLAUDE (1981) *Mythology. Volume 4 The Naked Man.* London: Jonathan Cape.
LODGE, DAVID (1977) *The Modes of Modern Writing.* Ithaca, NY.: Cornell University Press.
LODGE, DAVID (1981) *Working with Structuralism: Essays and Reviews on Nineteenth and Twentieth Century Fiction.* London: Routledge and Kegan Paul.
LURIE, ALISON (1982) *The Language of Clothes.* London: Heinemann.
LYONS, JOHN (1973) 'Structuralism in linguistics', in ROBEY, DAVID (ed.) *Structuralism: An Introduction.* Oxford: Clarendon Press.
MAGEE, BRIAN (ed.) (1978) *Men of Ideas.* London: British Broadcasting Corporation.
MARTIN, BERENICE (1981) *A Sociology of Contemporary Cultural Change.* Oxford: Basil Blackwell.
MATHIESON, M. (1975) *The Preachers of Culture.* London: Allen and Unwin.
McINTYRE, A. G. (1969) *Marxism and Christianity.* London: Duckworth.
MILLS, ROGER (1978) *A Comprehensive Schooling 1965–75.* London: Centreprise Trust.
MOGDIL, JOHAN and CELIA (1976) *Piagetian Research: Compilation and Commentary. Volume 1.* Windsor: National Foundation for Educational Research.
MUSGRAVE, P. W. (1968) *The School as an Organisation.* London: Macmillan.
NORRIS, CHRISTOPHER (1982) *Deconstruction.* London: Methuen.
NORRIS, CHRISTOPHER (1983) 'Mortal scripts'. *London Review of Books,* 5, 7, pp. 20–1.
OPEN UNIVERSITY. CURRICULUM DESIGN AND DEVELOPMENT COURSE TEAM (1976) *Case Study 3: Stantonbury Campus.* Milton Keynes: Open University Press.
OPEN UNIVERSITY. CURRICULUM EVALUATION AND ASSESSMENT IN EDUCATIONAL INSTITUTIONS COURSE TEAM (1982) *Case Study 2: Stantonbury Campus.* Milton Keynes: Open University Press.
ORMELL, CHRISTOPHER (1980) 'Values in Education', in STRAUGHAN, ROGER and WRIGLEY, JACK (eds) *Values and Evaluation in Education.* New York: Harper and Row.
PEEL, E. A. (1968) *The Pupil's Thinking.* London: Oldbourne.
PETERS, MICHAEL (1981) 'The English Teacher and Structuralism'. *The Times Educational Supplement,* 2 October 1981.
PIAGET, JEAN (1929) *The Child's Conception of the World.* London: Routledge and Kegan Paul; also published in paperback (1976) by Collins (Fontana).
PIAGET, JEAN (1971) *Structuralism.* London: Routledge and Kegan Paul.

POPPER, KARL (1968) *The Logic of Scientific Discovery* (revised edition). London: Hutchinson.

RICHARDS, I. A. (1929) *Practical Criticism: A Study of Literary Judgement*. London: Routledge and Kegan Paul.

ROBEY, DAVID (ed.) (1973) *Structuralism: An Introduction*. Oxford: Clarendon Press.

RUNCIMAN, W. G. (1983) *A Treatise on Social Theory. Volume 1 The Methodology of Social Theory*. Cambridge: Cambridge University Press.

RUTHERFORD, JOHN (1977) 'Structuralism', in ROUTH, J. and WOLFF, J. (eds) *The Sociology of Literature: Theoretical Approaches. Sociological Review Monograph 23*. Newcastle-under-Lyme: University of Keele (pp. 43–56).

RUTTER, MICHAEL, MAUGHAN, BARBARA, MORTIMORE, PETER and OUSTON, JANET (1979) *Fifteen Thousand Hours: Secondary Schools and their Effects on Children*. Shepton Mallet: Open Books.

SAUSSURE, FERDINAND DE (1974) *Course in General Linguistics* (translated by BASKIN, WADE). London: Collins (Fontana); first published 1916 and edited by BALLY, CHARLES and SECHEHAYE, ALBERT.

SCHOLES, ROBERT (1974) *Structuralism in Literature*. New Haven, Conn.: Yale University Press.

SCHUTZ, ALFRED (1967) *Phenomenology of the Social World*. Evanston, Ill.: Northwestern University Press.

SHARP, RACHEL *et al.* (1981) 'A case study of secondary schooling'. *British Journal of Sociology of Education*, 2, 3, pp. 275–91.

SHARP, RACHEL and GREEN, ANTHONY (1975) *Education and Social Control*. London: Routledge and Kegan Paul.

SMITH, JOHN MAYNARD (1982) 'Understanding science'. *London Review of Books*, 4, 10, p. 12.

SQUIBB, P. (1981) 'A theoretical structuralist approach to special education', in BARTON, LEN and TOMLINSON, SALLY (eds) *Special Education: Policy, Practices and Social Issues*. New York: Harper and Row.

STANWORTH, MICHELLE (1983) *Gender and Schooling*. London: Hutchinson.

STRICKLAND, GEOFFREY (1981) *Structuralism or Criticism? Thoughts on how we read*. Cambridge: Cambridge University Press.

SWINGEWOOD, A. (1976) *The Novel and Revolution*. London: Macmillan.

TAWNEY, R. H. (1926) *Religion and the Rise of Capitalism*. London: John Murray; also published in paperback (1969) by Penguin Books.

TODOROV, TZVETAN (1973) 'The structural analysis of literature', in ROBEY, DAVID (ed.) *Structuralism: An Introduction*. Oxford: Clarendon Press.

TOMLINSON, SALLY (1981) 'The social construction of the ESN(M) child', in BARTON, LEN and TOMLINSON, SALLY (eds) *Special Education: Policy, Practices and Social Issues*. New York: Harper and Row.

TOMLINSON, SALLY (1982) *A Sociology of Special Education*. London: Routledge and Kegan Paul.

TURNER, GLEN (1983) *The Social World of the Comprehensive School*. London: Croom Helm.

WALKER, STEPHEN and BARTON, LEN (eds) (1983) *Gender, Class and Education*. London: Falmer Press.

WARD, AILEEN (1963) *John Keats: The Making of a Poet*. London: Mercury Books.

WATSON, GEORGE (1978) *Modern Literary Thought*. Heidelberg: Carl Winter.

WEBER, MAX (1904) *The Protestant Ethic and the Spirit of Capitalism*. Reprinted (1952) London: Allen and Unwin.

WEINER, MARTIN J. (1981) *English Culture and the Decline of the Industrial Spirit 1850–1980*. Cambridge: Cambridge University Press.

WERTHEIMER, MAX (1961) *Productive Thinking*. London: Tavistock.

WHITE, ROGER and BROCKINGTON, DAVID (1983) *Tales out of School*. London: Routledge and Kegan Paul.

WILLIAMS, RAYMOND (1961) *The Long Revolution*. London: Chatto and Windus; also published in paperback (1965) by Penguin Books.

WILLIAMS, RAYMOND (1973) *Drama from Ibsen to Brecht*. Harmondsworth: Penguin Books.

WILLIAMS, RAYMOND (1977) *Marxism and Literature*. Oxford: Oxford University Press.

WILLIAMS, RAYMOND (1980) *Problems in Materialism and Culture*. London: Verso/New Left Books.

WILLIS, PAUL (1977) *Learning to Labour*. Aldershot: Saxon House.

WITTGENSTEIN, L. (1972) *Philosophical Investigations*. Oxford: Basil Blackwell.

WOODS, P. and HAMMERSLEY, M. (1977) *School Experience*. London: Croom Helm.

Index

absence, 17, 55, 56, 132
accessibility, 51
accommodation, 4, 35
accountability, 55, 76–9
achievement, 65, 67*ff*, 79
Adorno, T., 60
aesthetics, 32
agency, 18, 42, 138–42
Althusser, L., 25, 29, 50–60, 99, 109, 132, 143
Anderson, C., 49
anthropology, 2, 6, 11, 12, 38–44, 58, 111
Apple, M., 134
arbitrary character of the sign, 15, 20–1, 24, 25, 27, 29, 95, 101
Assessment of Performance Unit, 85
assimilation, 4, 35
associative, 46
astronomy, 9, 26
Atkinson, P., 115

Balibar, E., 60
Ball, S. J., 50, 80, 81, 86
Barton, L., 50, 87, 134–5
Barthes, R., 2, 11, 13, 19, 25, 29, 99, 104
Beachside Comprehensive, 58, 130
'bearers', 57, 58, 140
Becker, H. S., 80, 86
Belsey, C., 99, 104
Benveniste, E., 102
Berger, P., 86
Bernstein, B.B., 5, 9, 11, 13, 50, 106, 115–30, 134
binary oppositions, 37–43, 96, 125
biology, 8, 9, 11, 16, 131
Bloom, H., 101, 104
Boden, M.A., 45
Boulton, M., 103
Bowles, S., 54, 109–10, 134
Brockington, D., 86
Bruner, J.S., 152, 154

Calvinism, 65
Cambridge Accountability Project, 76–9
Cambridge University, 1, 12, 88, 93
Centre for Contemporary Cultural Studies, 87, 91
Chomsky, N., 4, 11, 13, 27, 31–2
Clarke, S., 46
classification, 5, 38, 45, 117–29
code, 5, 9, 10, 38, 41, 42, 101, 115–29
communication, 19
community, 62, 64, 72–3, 76–8
competence, 17–18, 27–8, 34, 42, 59, 64, 66, 77, 102, 129, 130–3, 136–53
competition, 70–2
concrete operations, 35
conventional structuralism, 106–10
Course in General Linguistics, 14, 29
Cowan, Q.A., 45
culinary triangle, 40–1
Culler, J., 2, 12, 18, 22, 29, 93, 95, 97–8, 103–4, 135
curriculum, 19, 32, 50, 55, 69, 71–2, 75–6, 88, 115–29, 131, 133–4, 153
curriculum criticism, 146, 153–4

Dale, R., 49, 134
Darwinian biology, 9
decentring the subject, 9–10, 23, 25, 27, 49, 94, 98–9, 105, 113, 129
deconstruction, 94, 99–102
democracy, 51, 62, 77*ff*, 105
definition of the situation, 83
Derrida, J., 25, 29, 94, 97, 99, 100, 103–4
Descartes, R., 26
de-schooling, 67
developmentalism, 82, 111
Dewey, J., 76
diachronic, 10, 15, 23–5, 28
difference, 21–3, 25
Donaldson, M., 45
Donoghue, D., 101

Douglas, M., 134
Durkheim, E., 14, 37, 47, 48, 108–9

Eagleton, T., 91, 103
economism, 52ff
Elliott, J., 154
embeddedness, 51, 56–7, 79, 85, 90, 108, 132–3
Engels, F., 53, 60
ethnography, 24, 111
ethos, school and classroom, 62, 67–75
event, 15, 17, 55, 56, 66, 136, 139
Evans, K.M., 50
existentialists, 52
expressive causality, 55

feeling, structures of, 28, 61–87, 130–1, 133, 137–53
Fiske, J., 135
Floud, J., 49
Ford, J., 113–15, 134–5
formal operations, 35
forms of knowledge, 32
Foucault, M., 104
framing, 117–29
Frankfurt School, 52, 57, 59–60, 83–4, 87
Frazer, Sir James, 41
Freud, S., 14, 38, 56, 72
Freudianism, 6, 9, 54, 56, 104
Friel, B., 145, 153
Froebel, F., 45, 82
Fromm, E., 60

Gadamer, H.G., 25, 29
Garbo, Greta, 2–3, 9–10, 19
Gellner, E., 32, 45
gestalt, 30–1, 44, 50
Geuss, R., 87
Gibson, R., 86, 148, 154
Giddens, A., 29, 58, 60, 64, 66, 86, 139, 141, 153
Gintis, H., 54, 109–10, 134
Goldmann, L., 102, 103–4, 147, 154
Grace, G., 79, 86
Green, Andre, 104
Green, Anthony, 50, 112, 134
Gronlund, N.E., 50

Habermas, J., 84
Halsey, A.H., 49, 108–9, 134
Hammersley, M., 29, 50
Hargreaves, D., 50, 75, 86
Harris, K., 109–10, 134
Hartley, J., 135
Hartman, G., 104
Heath, A.F., 134
Hegel, G.W.F., 30, 37, 55

Heideggerian, 104
Held, D., 59, 87
Hepburn, Audrey, 2–3, 9
Hillis Miller, J., 104
Hirst, P.H., 32, 45
Holland, J., 134
homology, 102, 147, 154
Horkheimer, M., 60
humanism, 52
Hume, D., 7
Husserl, E., 86

Ideological State Apparatus (ISA), 54, 59
ideology, 52ff, 62, 67, 79, 82–5, 92, 108, 110–11, 122, 143, 145
independence, 68, 77
individualism, 26, 62, 64, 72, 76–9, 82, 111–12
innocence, childhood, 82–3, 111
instrumental rationality, 60, 83–5
Isaacs, Susan, 45, 82

Jakobson, R., 4, 37, 40, 42, 94, 96, 103
Jay, M., 87
Jones, L., 103
Josipovici, G., 95, 103
Judaism, 62

Kant, I., 30, 31, 32
Karabel, J., 49
Karol, K.S., 59
Keats, John, 147, 154
Kermode, F., 93, 101, 103
Kettle, A., 91
King, R., 67, 82–3, 86, 111–12, 134
kinship, 38, 45
Koffka, K., 30
Köhler, W., 30–1, 50
Kristeva, J., 98, 103
Krylov, B., 60
Kuhn, T.S., 25, 29, 144, 153
Kurzweil, E., 29

Lacan, J., 25, 29
language, 5, 8–11, 14–29, 31, 36, 49–50, 57, 84, 102, 115ff, 132–3, 142, 144ff
language codes, 5, 117–29
langue, 14–18, 27–9, 38, 42, 46, 55, 57, 95, 98, 132, 139–40
Lavers, A., 104
Lawton, D., 36, 45, 131, 153
Leach, E., 2, 12, 38–41, 46
leadership styles, 51
Leavis, F.R., 89–94, 97, 101, 103
Leitch, V.B., 104
Lenin, N., 54

Levi-Strauss, C., 3, 9, 11, 13, 21, 26, 30, 32–3, 36–44, 46–8, 54, 59, 106, 115, 123, 125
Lewin, K., 50–1
linguistics, linguists, 4, 6, 13–15, 17, 19, 24–5, 33, 40, 117–29
literary criticism, 6, 146
literature, 8, 13, 25, 62, 88–104, 142, 146–7
Lippitt, R.N., 51
Locke, J., 7
Lodge, D., 93–4, 99, 101, 103
logic, 32
Lowenthal, L., 60
Luckmann, T., 86
Lurie, A., 135
Lyons, J., 4, 9, 11, 13

Magee, B., 45
Man, P. de, 104
Marcuse, H., 60, 84
Martin, B., 135
Marx, K., 37, 47, 48, 51, 65, 91
Marxism, Marxist, 6, 9, 11, 21, 24, 37, 49–59, 62–3, 67, 69, 84, 91–2, 101–2, 109–10, 112, 118, 142
mathematics, 6, 8, 10, 11, 25, 32, 33, 131, 153
Mathieson, M., 103
Mauss, M., 37
Maxwell, J., 31
McCabe, C., 1, 88, 93
McIntyre, A.G., 52
McMillan, Margaret and Rachel, 82
'medical model', 114
Merleau-Ponty, M., 52, 57
metonymic causality, 55
Mills, R., 29
Mogdil, J. and Mogdil, C., 45
Mongon, D., 134
Montessori, M., 82
moral understanding, 32
music, 30, 38–9, 46, 54
mythology, myth, 3, 8, 38–44, 95

natural attitude, 65, 86
negative capability, 147
Nietzche, F., 104
Norris, C., 104

Open University, 110
Ormell, C., 81–2, 86
over-determination, 53–6, 143

paradigmatic, 46
parity of esteem, 71

parole, 14–18, 27–9, 42, 46, 55, 57, 139–40
Parsons, T., 47, 48
pastoral care, 72, 77
Paulin, T., 12
Peel, E. A., 45
perspectives, 80
Pestalozzi, J.H., 45, 82
Peters, M., 103
phenomenology, 52, 65, 141
philosophy, 6, 30, 32
physics, 25
Piaget, J., 3, 7–11, 13, 23, 30, 32–7, 42, 44–6, 48, 51, 55, 72, 76, 97, 105, 132
Plato, 30
play, 45, 82, 111
Plowden Report, 82, 108
Planck, M., 31
Popper, K., 144, 153
presence, 17, 55, 132
post-structuralism, 93, 99–102
practical consciousness, 42, 64–7
practical criticism, 10–11, 89–90, 92, 146–7
process structuralism, 106, 110–15
professionalism, 64, 77
progressive education, 34, 112
Protestant ethic, 64–5, 74
psychiatry, 6
psychoanalysis, 54
psychology, 6, 25, 33

rationality, 69, 73, 74
reciprocity, 18, 59, 136–53
reference, 19, 25, 27, 43–4, 102, 138, 142–8
relationships, 8–9, 11–12, 15–16, 19–20, 22–5, 27–8, 40, 49, 53, 55, 94, 97–8, 105, 112, 117–29, 133, 139ff
relativism, 21, 27, 83, 100, 115
religion, 25
religious understanding, 32
Repressive State Apparatus, 59
Richards, I.A., 11, 13, 89–90, 103
Ridge, S.M., 134
Robbins Report, 85, 107–9
'Romantic theories', 45
Rousseau, J.J., 37, 45, 76
Runciman, W.G., 136–7
Rutherford, J., 97, 103–4
Rutter, M., 80–1, 86

Sartre, J-P., 52, 57
Saussure, F. de, 10, 12, 14–30, 46, 48, 55, 57, 95, 98, 132, 139
Scholes, R., 12, 13
Schutz, A., 64, 86

science, 5, 6, 9, 30, 32, 92, 142–4, 151
science, social, 6, 33
Searle, J., 15
self-regulation, 10–12, 34, 49, 94–6, 140*ff*
semiology, 18–19, 25, 27, 134
sensori-motor stage, 35
Shakespeare, W., 21, 88, 89, 90, 96, 100,
    147
Sharp, R., 50, 58, 60, 112, 134
sign, signifier and signified, 14, 18–21, 24,
    100, 134
Smith, J.M., 13
social formation, 53
social organisation, structures of, 28,
    47–60, 130–1, 133, 137–53
social welfare, 67, 72*ff*
sociology, 9, 25
sociology of education, 49, 115, 117
sociometry, 50
spontaneity, 67, 73*ff*
Squibb, P., 113, 134
Stantonbury, 153–4
Stanworth, M., 87
Strickland, G., 93, 103–4
structural analysis, 28–9, 102, 106, 130–4,
    136–53
structural causality, 53, 55, 132
Swingewood, A., 103
synchronic, 10, 11, 14, 15, 23–5, 28, 49,
    94, 98, 140
syntagmatic, 46

Tawney, R.H., 86
Thomas, W.I., 83

thought, structures of, 28, 30–46, 66,
    130–1, 133, 137–53
Todorov, T., 96, 97, 103
Tomlinson, S., 21, 113–14, 134–5
totemism, 38
transformation, 10–12, 16, 34, 36, 43,
    48–9, 54–5, 94, 96–7, 123, 133, 140*ff*
Turner, G., 51

valency, 51
vraisemblance, 95

Walker, S., 50, 87
Ward, A., 154
Warnock Report, 112, 134
Watson, G., 102, 104
Weber, M., 65, 86
Weightman, J. and Weightman, D., 45
Weiner, M.J., 86
Wertheimer, M., 30, 44
Whelan, M., 134
White, R., 86
White, R.K., 51
wholeness, wholes, 8, 11, 16, 20, 30, 36–7,
    47–56, 63, 81, 94–5, 102, 105, 131–2,
    139*ff*
Williams, R., 61–4, 86, 91–2, 103, 111,
    147, 154
Willis, P., 29, 50, 75, 79–81, 86, 111–12,
    134
Wittgenstein, L., 15, 22, 25, 29
Woods, P., 29, 50
Wragg, E., 85